6

THE MISSION OF THE CHURCH AND THE PROPAGATION OF THE FAITH

THE MISSION OF THE CHURCH
AND THE PROPAGATION
OF THE FAITH

PAPERS READ AT
THE SEVENTH SUMMER MEETING AND
THE EIGHTH WINTER MEETING
OF THE
ECCLESIASTICAL HISTORY SOCIETY

EDITED BY
G. J. CUMING

CAMBRIDGE
AT THE UNIVERSITY PRESS
1970

Published by the Syndics of the Cambridge University Press
Bentley House, 200 Euston Road, London N.W.1
American Branch: 32 East 57th Street, New York, N.Y.10022

© Cambridge University Press 1970

Library of Congress Catalogue Card Number: 77-108105

Standard Book Number: 521 07752 4

Printed in Great Britain
at the University Printing House, Cambridge
(Brooke Crutchley, University Printer)

PREFACE

It is a pleasure to record the gratitude of the Ecclesiastical History Society to the Syndics of the Cambridge University Press, who have undertaken the publication of this series of *Studies in Church History*, for the next three years in the first instance. It is our warm hope that this will prove the beginning of a long and happy collaboration. The volumes will have at their centre, as in recent years, a major theme in the history of the Church, and will continue to represent the Society at work by consisting mainly of papers read and discussed at its Conferences.

It is a pleasure, too, to record our gratitude to Messrs E. J. Brill of Leiden, whose kindness made possible the publication of volumes III, IV and V. We are sorry to part from them, and they from us.

'The Mission of the Church and the Propagation of the Faith' was the theme of the seventh summer meeting (at the University of Sussex) and of the eighth winter meeting of the Society. Most of the papers included in this volume were read at one or the other of these meetings, but three relevant papers from earlier meetings have been added. The papers are arranged in chronological order of subject-matter.

The untimely death of Dr G. S. M. Walker deprived the Society of the opportunity of hearing his communication on St Columban, but fortunately the paper was fully prepared for publication, and we are particularly glad to be able to include it.

We should like to take this opportunity of drawing attention to the parallel study by Professor W. H. C. Frend, 'The Missions of the Early Church, 180–700 A.D.', which is to appear in the Proceedings of the Comité Internationale d'Histoire Ecclésiastique Comparative, Conference of 1968, and complements the papers printed here.

C. N. L. Brooke
President
G. J. Cuming
Editor

ACKNOWLEDGEMENTS

The paper by C. R. Boxer is from *The Portuguese Seaborne Empire 1415–1825*. Copyright © 1969 by C. R. Boxer; reprinted by kind permission of Alfred A. Knopf, Inc. and of the Hutchinson Publishing Group.

CONTENTS

CONTRIBUTORS

L. G. D. BAKER, Lecturer in Medieval History, University of Edinburgh

C. R. BOXER, Professor of the History of the Expansion of Europe Overseas, Yale University

C. N. L. BROOKE, Professor of History, Westfield College, London

PETER HINCHLIFF, formerly Professor of Ecclesiastical History, Rhodes University, South Africa

G. HUELIN, Lecturer, Theological Department, King's College, London

R. A. MARKUS, Senior Lecturer in Medieval History, University of Liverpool

S. C. NEILL, formerly Professor of Missions and Ecumenical Theology, University of Hamburg

C. H. TALBOT, Medievalist at Wellcome Institute of the History of Medicine, London

A. P. VLASTO, Lecturer in Slavonic Studies, University of Cambridge

The late G. S. M. WALKER, formerly Senior Lecturer in Church History and Doctrine, University of Leeds

A. F. WALLS, Senior Lecturer in Church History, University of Aberdeen

THE MISSION OF SS. CYRIL AND METHODIOS AND ITS AFTERMATH IN CENTRAL EUROPE

by A. P. VLASTO

THE achievement of SS. Cyril and Methodios may be summarized as follows: in 863 the Byzantine emperor sent to the Prince of Moravia, at the latter's request, a mission led by the brother saints to develop the evangelization of his lands, since Frankish missionaries were becoming politically more and more *personae non gratae* in Moravia. By the time that the surviving brother Methodios died in 885, as archbishop and papal legate in Moravia, the principle of the mission had not only been maintained in the face of constant opposition but also accepted, if only partially and grudgingly, elsewhere. This principle was that any people, especially neophyte, must be allowed to praise God in its own language: only through one's native tongue can one fully understand the promises of baptism, the liturgy, and the Holy Scriptures. During those twenty years a form of the Slav language was elevated to literary status and recorded in a specially designed alphabet, and many clerks had been trained in it. From Moravia its use spread first to those lands which came under Moravian rule in the 870s and 880s—Bohemia, Pannonia, and (very probably) south Poland. On Methodios's death the Frankish clergy regained the upper hand in Moravia and dispersed the saints' colleagues and disciples, who then found support for their ministry in yet other Slav lands, namely Croatian Dalmatia and Bulgaria.

The Cyrillomethodian principle was a purely linguistic one. The *Lives* of SS. Cyril and Methodios and the earliest surviving Slav texts make it clear enough that during their lifetimes the bulk of translation was done from Greek liturgical and biblical texts; but it is also clear that the brothers had no intention of suppressing or limiting the concurrent use of Latin texts nor of forbidding their translation into Slav, for Latin Christianity was already established in Moravia, Slovakia, and Pannonia before 863.

The evidence is not sufficient to estimate the proportion in actual use of Greek and Latin liturgies, both in Slav translation, in Moravia and its dependencies, but the work of Cyrillomethodian refugees in their new fields after 885 points to the same readiness to fall in with whatever best furthered Christian life in those parts, namely to adopt the more or less exclusive use of Slav versions of the Latin Mass in Bohemia and Dalmatia, but of the Greek liturgy in Bulgaria. Further, the original script, St Cyril's own invention, later called the Glagolitic alphabet, continued to be used in Bohemia and Dalmatia, but was soon rejected in most of Bulgaria in favour of an alphabet more closely modelled on the Greek, the so-called Cyrillic, which took shape there in the last decade of the ninth century.

It had been touch and go whether this Slav ecclesiastical language would survive its infancy. Papal support was probably decisive. The Franks were always opposed to it. It was Wiching, Bishop of Nitra under Methodios but a Latinophile Frank, who in 885 engineered the expulsion of those who adhered to the Cyrillomethodian principle. We do not know how complete this expulsion was nor how rigorous the suppression of Church Slavonic (as it is commonly called) throughout the Moravian state. Consequently it is difficult to pronounce, in default of explicit documents, on the subsequent practice of the Moravian Church, especially after about 898, when Pope John IX agreed to the restoration of the archbishopric with three subordinate sees. It is not even perfectly clear that this independent hierarchy was fully established.

Then came the irruption of the Magyars. By 906 they had destroyed the Moravian state, bringing Christian institutions to the verge of extinction. Bohemia and south Poland alone were beyond the limits of their conquest. It is, however, probable that the more mountainous parts of Moravia and Slovakia escaped the worst of their ravages, being country unattractive to steppe horsemen; here and there Christian communities may have survived the débâcle. Moravia, the cradle of the Cyrillomethodian mission, remains a blank for half a century. Only after the Battle of the Lechfeld in 955 were the Magyars confined to the approximate boundaries of modern Hungary; thereafter the rehabilitation of Moravia and the evangelization of the Magyars themselves could be undertaken.

Our present concern is then, in what parts of Europe outside the Balkans did Church Slavonic survive in liturgical use? Were such communities mere scattered relics soon to perish, or were some sufficiently vigorous, not merely to maintain the practice and continue to train a Slav priesthood, but even to expand and form as it were a second wave of Cyrillomethodian missionary activity? There is a considerable divergence of opinions. Two scholars who advocate a high level of vitality of Church Slavonic in Central Europe, specifically in Poland, have fairly recently made known the results of their researches in English.[1] It is important therefore to try to give an impartial review of the question in the light of much other work published in Slav languages which may not be accessible to the English reader.

For much of Central Europe the tenth century is an obscure period about which the annals of more fortunate lands have little to say. Because of its closer involvement in German affairs the history of Bohemia alone is rather better illuminated. Here the Latin and Slav languages existed side by side in ecclesiastical use, if not from the adoption of Christianity by the rulers of Prague towards the end of the ninth century, then certainly from the time of St Wenceslas in the early tenth. Bohemian Christianity developed first under the aegis of Bavarian Regensburg. From 973, with the erection of the see of Prague, and its inclusion in the archdiocese of Mainz, Bohemia's political and ecclesiastical life was more and more dominated by the Empire. Yet the use of Church Slavonic held its own, indeed became more vigorous towards the end of the tenth century, apparently under the

[1] K. Lanckorońska, *Studies on the Roman-Slavonic rite in Poland* (Rome 1961; = *Orientalia Christiana Analecta* 161); H. Paszkiewicz, *The Making of the Russian Nation* (London 1963), developing his earlier *The Origin of Russia* (London 1954).

1-2

encouragement of the Czech St Adalbert as bishop of Prague, and was not seriously threatened until the middle of the eleventh century. Papal and Imperial pressure then brought about its suppression within the next fifty years.

The survival of the Cyrillomethodian principle in Bohemia is a well-authenticated fact. But how far can we go with the extreme partisans of a 'Cyrillomethodian theory' in their belief that Church Slavonic found a no less favourable soil in south and east Poland, that Christianity in those parts so flourished in its Slav form as to lead to the creation of a separate Cyrillomethodian metropolis in south Poland, at least in the first quarter of the eleventh century, and to project its influence even as far east as Kiev?

The geographical aspect of this conception is in itself favourable. At its greatest extension in the 880s the Great Moravian State had embraced Bohemia, south Poland and an indefinite area further east, reaching towards the purely Russian lands. More important, one of the great trade-routes of tenth-century Europe linked the three towns of Prague, Cracow, and Kiev. Trade follows the flag; it is no less true that missionary activity follows trade.

Let us first examine Poland. The early spread of Christianity to south Poland can be accepted. For the tenth century this is confirmed by the earliest strata of building on the Wawel (or citadel) of Cracow and from archaeological evidence elsewhere in the Upper Vistula valley. We may even accept Methodian missions from the late 870s, as suggested in the *Vita Methodii*, but absolute continuity from this early date falls short of proof. But it does not follow that such missions necessarily involved the propagation of Church Slavonic: the earliest of all may rather have been entrusted to the Latinophile Wiching. Similarly, during the short-lived restoration of the Moravian Church during the first years of the tenth century, which may have envisaged and possibly even established a bishopric at Cracow, the availability of priests and teachers in Church Slavonic is problematical. Against this, though some of the refugees from Moravia may well have settled in south Poland after 885, none of the five chief disciples known by name did so: to be exact, four established themselves in Bulgaria, and the fate of the fifth is unknown.[1] In the course of the tenth century south Poland became, owing to its central position on the important trade-route, a bone of contention between Prague and the new state of Poland in process of formation to the north, whose centres were Gniezno and Poznań. Cracow changed hands several times, to be permanently attached to Poland only from the very end of the tenth century.

The first ruler of central Poland to be baptized, Mieszko, received Christianity together with a Christian wife from Prague in 965. Nothing in the meagre records suggests that this was not an extension of the Latin Church. But clearly the use of Church Slavonic in some measure can never be excluded in the tenth century from Bohemian work and the same applies to evangelization which may have been carried out by Bohemians in the disputed lands in between—south Poland and Silesia. There is some far from reliable evidence of bishops at Cracow, possibly also at Silesian Breslau, before the year 1000, but no clear indication to what hierarchy they belonged or what liturgical language they favoured. The little that is known of the diocese of Prague does not help to resolve the uncertainty: we have nothing but a tendentious document of 1086 claiming that its jurisdiction had originally extended over south Poland and lands even further east—a specious claim obviously motivated by Prague's pretensions to aggrandizement at a moment when the Bohemian and Polish crowns were temporarily united. It is far more probable that the diocese of Prague was confined to Bohemia, with the occasional addition of Moravia and conceivably Cracow when it was in Czech hands. On any showing, then, a stable bishopric at Cracow, especially one serving as a Church Slavonic centre, is a very frail assumption. The most that we can say is that the language may have been used by some Christians in south Poland.

[1] It has been suggested (see Z. Dittrich, *Christianity in Great Moravia*) that this fifth disciple, Gorazd, whom Methodios intended as his successor, did in fact become Archbishop of Moravia about 899 when the Pope restored the hierarchy; and further, that he withdrew on the Magyar conquest to south Poland (Cracow?), where he was able to develop Christianity in Cyrillomethodian form. This is held to account for the appearance of Gorazd in a late Polish calendar from Wiślica. Both points are quite unsubstantiated and remain nothing more than interesting speculations.

In contrast the history of Mieszko's Poland is tolerably clear. There is no good reason to doubt the so-called Donation of Poland to the Holy See in 992, a move designed to counter continuing German ambitions to dominate the country both politically and ecclesiastically. It was followed in the year 1000 by the creation of the Latin archbishopric of Gniezno, the fruit of Otto III's political wisdom and veneration for his martyred friend, St Adalbert of Prague. This was an act agreed at the highest level between the Emperor, the Pope, and Bolesław of Poland. Gniezno became both capital and primatial see. The bishopric of Poznań was left for the moment on one side not, as some have contended, because it came under Magdeburg, but because this had been hitherto the original Polish missionary bishopric and its incumbent could not be persuaded to accept what he regarded as a curtailment of his rights. Under Gniezno were placed Latin bishoprics of Cracow and Breslau for the provinces of Little Poland and Silesia respectively, which were by then at least semi-Christian; and, more hopefully, a bishopric for the still largely pagan Pomeranians at Kolberg on the Baltic, which was found within a very few years not to be viable. But Polish lands now extended a long way east till they met those of Vladimir of Kiev somewhere in Galicia. Why was no further provision made? The more cautious historian concludes that the eastern lands were still almost untouched by Christianity and did not yet rate even the consideration given to Pomerania: the dioceses of Gniezno and Cracow were left with indefinite eastern limits. Partisans of the 'Cyrillomethodian theory' would have us believe that there already existed in those parts one or more flourishing Cyrillomethodian sees, even a metropolis, which it was considered impolitic or impossible to displace. Yet the fact is nowhere mentioned. It is difficult to see any good reasons why any of the three parties to the Act of Gniezno should have objected to the use of the Slav ecclesiastical language in part of the Polish Church—Otto as the friend of the Slav Adalbert who, as Bohemian history makes clear, was certainly no narrow Latinophile; Bolesław as an empire-builder who hoped to enlarge, and did for a short time enlarge, the Polish state by the conquest of Bohemia and Moravia;

6

and the Pope as one who is not known to have attacked the use of Church Slavonic either in Bohemia or Dalmatia. If Bolesław and his father Mieszko had tolerated this use in Poland, what need for a separate metropolis for the Slavophiles and why this improbable silence? Would not also that loyal Saxon, Bishop Thietmar of Merseburg, with his bias against Poland and indeed against all Slavs, who was loath even to accept a Latin Polish Church independent of the Empire as legitimate, have had something derogatory to say about an even more strongly Slav ecclesiastical body? Yet he is one of the few contemporary sources who tells us about Gniezno in some detail.

The alleged evidence is all of later date and highly circumstantial. On the death of Bolesław in 1025 Poland went through a period of profound internal disorder. To this can be conveniently ascribed all the deficiencies of our sources. Later Latin chroniclers tend to attribute these civil wars to the revolt of the still pagan parts of east Poland. Here we are right to be suspicious, for the so-called 'Anonymus Gallus' also speaks of 'falsi christicolae' and of those 'a fide catholica deviantes'. This could not be said of pagans, but much more credibly of Cyrillomethodians who were obstinately defending their use of Church Slavonic. We have also to reckon with his statement that at the time of Bolesław's death there were two metropolitan sees in Poland. This is apparently supported by Master Vincent about a century later, who alludes to Bolesław's 'gemina metropolis'. But the passage is not altogether clear and probably also not independent of the earlier writer.

The first point supports what there is no call to deny, that Christians using Church Slavonic were to be found in south and probably east Poland, deriving the use either direct from Moravia or from Bohemia. But few will go all the way with Paszkiewicz in seeing the rebellious Masław of Mazovia as the champion of a large body of staunch Cyrillomethodians resisting Latin uniformity in the eastern provinces, whose cultural level at this time can scarcely have been comparable with central Poland, so much more strongly exposed to Bohemian and German influences.

The second point is, I believe, a misconception. Order was

7

gradually restored in Poland from the end of the 1030s, when Kazimierz, called the Restorer, imposed his rule with German military backing and summoned Western clergy in large numbers to reorganize the Church. During the troubles Gniezno had been destroyed. Cracow now became the chief town in Church and State. Kazimierz's primate, Aaron of Cologne, and his successors at Cracow, were thus the important figures until Gniezno was fully rehabilitated in 1136. The bald lists given in various Polish annals not infrequently confuse the names of Gniezno and Cracow prelates. It is a great deal more probable that Cracow has been unduly magnified in antiquity and dignity than that a Cyrillomethodian metropolis was constituted (how and by whom remains a mystery) at a place which neither the chronicles of Poland nor of any other country record. Cracow and Gniezno were two metropolitan sees, but not in fact at the same time.

Kazimierz was undoubtedly a Latinist; in the later eleventh century we should certainly expect a policy of Latin uniformity to be intensified, as in neighbouring Bohemia. Whether certain Polish rulers after him favoured Church Slavonic again, as some assert, is a question which cannot be pursued here. It is difficult to believe that its use was ever deep-rooted in Poland. Thus, not a single Church Slavonic manuscript of Polish provenance has survived, nor any evidence of the use of the Glagolitic alphabet there. Church Slavonic books were thoroughly purged from Bohemia by the Latinists at the end of the eleventh century, yet enough have survived, chiefly in Russian copies, to prove the vitality of the Cyrillomethodian tradition in Bohemia. It is at least odd then that they should have successfully travelled from Bohemia to Russia but not at all from Poland. Again, whereas Polish religious vocabulary contains not a few Church Slavonic words, they are all loans from Bohemia, whose spoken and written language for long exerted a considerable influence on Polish; there is no sign of direct loans from Moravian, or for that matter Russian, Church Slavonic. In other words, one can adduce no linguistic facts to demonstrate that the language was widely cultivated in Polish lands. Lastly it has yet to be proved, though it is likely, that here and there Church Slavonic was cultivated in Polish monasteries, as it was for example in the Benedictine house of Sázava near Prague, and less certainly at Břevnov and elsewhere. The foundation dates of Polish monasteries are very imperfectly known, their affiliation with Cyrillomethodian houses in Bohemia or Moravia not demonstrable. For this to be an important factor, we should have to show that, as in Bohemia, they could provide the training in Church Slavonic and the *scriptoria* without which the continuance of the Cyrillomethodian tradition in either country would have been problematical.

It is not possible here to evaluate every point brought in support of this theory. All the evidence is circumstantial, and it must be remembered that for Poland virtually all documentary evidence dates from after 1100, much of it long after. The danger in trusting later medieval references to Church Slavonic in Poland, and even in Bohemia, lies in the fourteenth-century revival of Slav letters in Bohemia under the patronage of Charles IV. He summoned Benedictines competent in Church Slavonic and the Glagolitic script from the one region where the Cyrillomethodian tradition was still alive in a Catholic church—Dalmatia. Earlier texts were rewritten and embellished, documents falsified to enhance the precocious Slav culture of the time of St Wenceslas, the national patron saint. The movement spread to Poland too, whose literature was still under Bohemian influence. We must therefore be wary of accepting at its face value any and every remark favourable to the theory. Where even circumstantial evidence is lacking it is easy to say that the rabid Latinists of the twelfth century and after were bent on suppressing all record of a hated rival. For there is an outstanding example of this attitude in Cosmas of Prague, who died in 1125: he does not so much as mention the coming of Church Slavonic to Bohemia nor its continued use there down to his own lifetime.

Let us now turn to Russia—to Kiev. Throughout the ninth–eleventh centuries Kiev was the centre of Russian culture. In reconstructing early Russian Christianity we have to rely mainly on Byzantine historians and Russian chronicles. There are in both what seem to us arbitrary omissions, which again have been held to suggest some deliberate reticence on one side or the other.

9

The first Greek approaches to Kiev date with high probability from the time of Patriarch Photios, whose wide-ranging missionary activity in support of Byzantine diplomacy in the 860s included the sending of SS. Cyril and Methodios to Moravia and the conversion of Bulgaria. But the military control of Kiev and the whole trade-route from the Baltic to Constantinople by pagan Scandinavians nullified or greatly reduced this promising start during the rest of the ninth century. Texts of commercial treaties with Constantinople in 911 and 944, which appear reliable, show that Christianity was rapidly gaining strength in Kiev during those decades; but there is no indication of who was responsible for the work. The critical moment comes, as in Poland, in the mid-tenth century. Olga, as regent for her son Svjatoslav from 945 to 962, was a Christian princess, whose reception in Constantinople in 957 is recorded by the Emperor Constantine Porphyrogenitus. She took her chaplain with her, but we do not know whether there was a bishop in Kiev then. Russia would have been recognized as a Christian state from that time, had it not been for the recalcitrance of her son Svjatoslav and the troubles which followed his death in 972. The final stage was reached when his son Vladimir, called to play a decisive part in Byzantine politics, was converted and imposed Christianity on his people in the years 987–9.

This seems a straightforward story. The most formative influences on the Russians came from the Greeks and the Bulgarians. Russia was drawn into various wars between Bulgaria and the Byzantine Empire from the last years of the ninth century; Russia aided and abetted the Empire in crushing the Bulgarian state in the 970s. It was from tenth-century Bulgaria, then at the height of its prosperity, that Russia received the Cyrillic alphabet—a Bulgarian invention—and the Slav liturgical language. There can be little doubt that both were known in Kiev from the beginnings of organized Christian life there in the earlier tenth century. Russian trading parties resided in Constantinople for several months each summer from at latest 944, but Greek influence was probably the lesser until the time of Vladimir's conversion. Unfortunately no Byzantine sources illuminate the process.

Why then should there be such imprecision about the baptism of both Olga and Vladimir? Russian sources are uncertain whether Olga was baptized in Constantinople or in Kiev, where there was certainly a church in the 950s, a church dedicated to the typically eastern St Elias. The Emperor Constantine does not mention baptism as the object of her elaborate reception in the Imperial City in 957 and refers to her by her pagan name Helga, not by her Christian name Helen. Yet she was certainly not baptized after 957. Greek-inspired Russian sources link Vladimir's baptism to his marriage to the Greek princess Anna in 989; other Russian sources appear to believe that he was baptized a year or so earlier in Kiev. One can understand the Greeks being jealous of their inveterate enemies the Bulgarians and glossing over their greater success in Kiev, in which the main factor was no doubt the use of the Slav language for Christian instruction and the provision of the sacred texts in Church Slavonic. It is less obvious why a Russian should refrain from stating that these two rulers received baptism at the hands of the Bulgarians, if this was the fact.

There is one further matter of controversy about which the sources are either silent or confused—the status of the Russian Church during the fifty years between Vladimir's baptism and the known arrival of a Greek metropolitan, consecrated in Constantinople, in the year 1039.

We should examine therefore whether there are any good grounds for supposing the Bulgarian influence not as strong as it appears and seeking links between Kiev and centres of Cyrillomethodian Christianity in the West. Accepting that Kiev early adopted the Cyrillomethodian principle of using the Slav language in the Church—and the Greeks as well as the Latins were often reluctant to approve this—the question resolves itself into this, did Latin or Orthodox rites prevail in Kiev in the tenth century, perhaps even into the early eleventh? Clearly both the Greeks and later Russian churchmen reared in the period of Greek ascendancy would be particularly apt to draw the veil over a Latin stage in Russian Christian development.

I have stressed the vitality of the trade-route from Kiev to Prague and beyond. Russian merchants are known as far afield as

Bavaria as early as the first decade of the tenth century. Kiev was then already a factor in European as well as Byzantine politics. A cultural current from Prague and Cracow to Kiev is perfectly admissible but one seeks in vain for evidence to support the view that it outweighed the influence of Bulgaria. It must suffice here to select one or two points.

Why did Olga approach Otto I in 959, a few years after her baptism, and Otto reply by sending the monk of Trier, Adalbert, as missionary bishop to Kiev in 961? Adalbert was a Slav speaker, to be elevated in 968, after the signal failure of his Russian mission, to the new archbishopric of Magdeburg. Otto was full of great plans after 955: Magdeburg was to be the spearhead of German missionary work among the Slavs of north Europe, paving the way for German territorial and economic expansion. Otto had hoped therefore to bring the infant Polish Church under his control, but the farsightedness of Mieszko and the prudence of the Curia in keeping the missionary bishopric of Poznań out of the clutches of the *Reichskirche* had successfully countered this plan. Conversely, Otto was able in 973 to bring the Bohemian Church firmly within it. A foothold in Kiev in 961 could be of inestimable value to his eastern policy. However we choose to interpret this incident, it can surely have no bearing on a 'Cyrillomethodian Church', for Adalbert was no representative of that. I should judge rather that Olga's approach was a political move motivated by her dissatisfaction with the negotiations which she personally led in Constantinople in 957, just as Boris of Bulgaria had turned to the Franks and to the Pope for missionaries soon after his formal acceptance of Orthodoxy in 864, being dissatisfied with the high-handed behaviour of Greek clergy in his country. We must not exaggerate the importance to these neophyte rulers of the precise form of Christianity which they adopted at a time when East and West were not formally divided: the political implications of their religious affiliations were of equal if not greater importance.

As the tenth century wore on, Kiev became more and more directly involved in Central European affairs. In 981 Vladimir extended his political control further west along the trade-route into Galicia. Was this another opening for Western usages at Kiev and a Western baptism for Vladimir? There is nothing concrete to support it. Certain minor Western traits are quite possible in Vladimir's ecclesiastical arrangements, but even those which look most plausible have not been proved beyond doubt, for example the inspiration of his so-called Tithe Church at Kiev, to which he allotted one-tenth of his revenues. Endowments of a similar kind were adopted on a number of later occasions in the eleventh and twelfth centuries; in no case was it a tithe in the Western sense.

Once again we must have recourse to linguistic evidence. The earliest surviving documents written in Russia date only from the middle of the eleventh century. They are in Cyrillic and show by this, and by the style of Church Slavonic used, manifest dependence on Bulgarian sources. The very scant epigraphic material from the tenth century is also in Cyrillic. The Glagolitic alphabet, the necessary vehicle of Central European texts, was known but had little currency in Russia; it is more likely that it came there from Macedonia than Central Europe. If there had been a substantial Western influence on the young Christian Church in Kiev, we should still be able to detect in the earliest Russian texts some traits at least of the distinctive style of Western Church Slavonic, possibly also some traces of Latin liturgical practice. There are none. Must we again fall back on the assumption that elimination and destruction in later Orthodox days was complete? The truth of the matter is that this Western influence was notably slight down to 989, and indeed into the early eleventh century. In contrast, from the founding of the monastery of Sázava near Prague about 1032 as a centre of Cyrillomethodian practice and training, until 1096 when it was finally reformed as a normal Latin house—a date which may be taken as the end of the Cyrillomethodian tradition in Bohemia—immediate repercussions are observable in Russia. Bohemian manuscripts reach Kiev and are there transliterated into Cyrillic; the cult of St Wenceslas is introduced; a few words of Western Church Slavonic do in fact now find their way into Russian usage. This was the time of close dynastic connections with Poland, Bohemia, and Hungary, deliberately pursued for political ends. But none of this affected the essential

Orthodoxy of the Russian Church, implanted as much by the Bulgarians as the Greeks.

Paszkiewicz tries to make much of the phrase 'slovenesk jazyk' (Slav tongue) in an account of early Russian history inserted in the *Russian Primary Chronicle* between about 1096 and 1113.[1] The chronicler writes: 'For the following alone are *slovenesk jazyk* in the land of Rus.' The list of Slav tribes then given omits one or two which were still obstinately pagan at the time he wrote. Paszkiewicz therefore proposes to give the phrase a religious connotation as 'Christians using the Slav liturgical language', or 'members of a Slav-language Church'. This would be parallel to the common later usage 'latinesk jazyk,' the Latin Christian world. Even if the religious interpretation of 'slovenesk jazyk' were acceptable in this context, this would imply nothing in itself in favour of a Western affiliation: as Orthodox Christians the Russians had long used Church Slavonic in its Bulgarian form. But the whole passage is about language and peoples, not churches: the learned monk lists the non-Slav peoples surrounding the land of Rus, each of which has its own language and all of whom were still pagan. That he omitted a couple of Slav-speaking tribes is surely pure oversight.

No one, I think, goes so far as to suggest that the Church in Kiev was formally subordinate to the hypothetical Cyrillomethodian metropolis in Poland in the early eleventh century. Moreover, there is in my opinion sufficient evidence to accept Kiev as a metropolis in the patriarchate of Constantinople from the time of Vladimir's marriage to Anna in 989. One person who could have cleared up for us once and for all this point and the whole question of Western practices at Kiev was St Bruno of Querfurt, who visited Kiev in 1008 on his way to evangelize the Pechenegs. But he says nothing.

Reference has been made to the connections between Sázava and Kiev. There were other links in the chain. The restoration of Christian life in those lands which the Magyars had barbarized is not well documented. The persistence of some Christian com-

[1] See *The Making of the Russian Nation*, ch. 2, recapitulating the arguments of *The Origin of Russia*, chs. 1–2.

munities in parts of Moravia, especially perhaps in the north about Olomouc, and in Slovakia (for example, at Nitra) remains uncertain. After 955 Bohemia occupied Moravia, and a bishopric separate from that of Prague appears to have existed there at least during part of the later tenth century. By the 990s the West, especially Bohemia and Bavaria, was playing the major part in the evangelization of the Magyars, though there was also a considerable Byzantine contribution. According to the legend, it was St Adalbert of Prague himself who baptized Vajk, the future St Stephen, who received a papal crown and archbishopric in 1000. By the eleventh century we can point with certainty to a number of monasteries in Moravia and Hungary which cultivated, like Sázava, Church Slavonic. Their central position favoured links with Bohemia, Poland, Croatia, and eastern Europe. We know little about them; their sources of Church Slavonic and liturgical practices were probably various. In this area too there is no sign of a Cyrillomethodian organization, whether an ancient one which had somehow survived the cataclysm, or a more recent revival. In the course of the eleventh century the Hungarian Church became gradually more and more purely Latin.

It is important to examine all the implications of this 'Cyrillomethodian theory' in order to convince oneself what scant attention has been paid by its advocates to the mechanics of church history—that is, to the conditions under which such Christian bodies can formally come into being and perpetuate themselves together with any peculiar practices which they may have. The very title of Lanckorońska's work, *Studies on the Roman-Slavonic rite in Poland*, invites misconception. There is not and there never has been a 'Slavonic rite' in the strict sense (as, for example, the Mozarabic rite)—merely Catholic and Orthodox rites performed in Church Slavonic. Again, if we look for a Cyrillomethodian *Church*—that is, a body with its own hierarchy—the only certain early example is that of Methodios himself from 870 to 885, as archbishop of Moravia and Pannonia in direct subordination to the Pope. It was for this autonomy that the Franks persecuted Methodios and his clergy, as well as for the (to them) unwarranted use of a barbarous dialect for sacred purposes. Methodios introduced no rites that did not already exist in Greek or Latin use. Perhaps we should add the Bulgarian Orthodox Church, which appears to have been autocephalous from about 870 but did not replace Greek by Church Slavonic for another quarter of a century.

The question of language is one thing and hierarchy another. If language had remained the sole criterion, then of course Bulgaria, Serbia, and Russia all had Cyrillomethodian churches sooner or later, and Bohemia and Croatian Dalmatia for a greater or lesser part of their history. The former were Orthodox, the latter Catholic. Only in Poland, a conspicuously Latin-Catholic country, is the use of Church Slavonic more problematical. We can accept that there were some 'Cyrillomethodian' Christians at least in parts of Poland down to 1000 and probably to a lesser degree for something like another century. What cannot be accepted on present evidence is that the Latinophiles and Slavophiles formed separate bodies with a separate hierarchy. The Moravian Church was not divided. Latin and Slav were used side by side in Bohemia for some two centuries not in two churches but in one. Latin and Slav were used side by side in the Dalmatian Church right into the twentieth century, with papal authority, in a purely Catholic church with a single hierarchy. I view the case of Poland in the same light. The existence of a Slav metropolis, even for a limited period, raises questions of the manner of its creation and the appointment and consecration of its hierarchs which do not seem to trouble its proponents. Moreover, however strong the animosity of the Latins against such an anomaly and however thorough their alleged attempts to cover up unwelcome facts, it is difficult to believe that no mention of its creation should anywhere survive in the records, fragmentary though they are, of such ecclesiastical centres as Prague, Cracow, Gniezno, and Kiev, whose affairs it could not but affect.

Further research must clearly be directed to the history of south Poland. But those who pursue it must beware of importing into the history of the tenth and early eleventh centuries too much incompatibility and that kind of intolerance which only came to the fore towards the end of the eleventh century after the Great Schism. They must also beware of constructing Uniate churches *ante factum.*

THE SHADOW OF THE CHRISTIAN SYMBOL

by L. G. D. BAKER

IN the year 1000 the Emperor Otto III went on a grandiose pilgrimage to Gnesen, to the tomb of his friend St Adalbert of Prague, martyred by the Prussians on the borders of their country on St George's Day, 997.[1] This visit has been seen as a significant moment in the development of the emperor's imperial policies, but it may also be taken to mark the end of the first great age in the history of Christendom. By the time that Otto came to pay his respects at the shrine of this Germanized Bohemian, St Vojtiekh,[2] and to raise it to metropolitan rank,[3] Europe was outwardly Christian. The tenth century had completed the process begun with the first urban apostolic missions, and had seen the absorption of the Viking settlers into the Christian community, the conversion of the Magyars, the establishment of the faith in Bohemia, Poland, Russia and Denmark, the beginnings of successful missionary activity in the more northerly Scandinavian lands, and the reconversion of Crete. Whatever problems might remain in Islamic Spain, or with the tenacious paganism of the eastern Baltic, by the year 1000 Europe was Christian, and the missionary millennium was over.

In this lengthy process the principal landmarks are clear. We know who the missionaries were; we have a hagiographical idea of their characters and achievements; we know where they worked and when, and the outlines of the ecclesiastical organizations which they established are apparent to us. Throughout the period a succession of great, and often eccentric, saints appear, and their labours are set in a common evangelical tradition which gives unity to the whole, long-drawn-out missionary endeavour. There

[1] F. Dvornik, *The Making of Central and Eastern Europe* (London 1949), pp. 131 ff.
[2] Ibid. p. 96.   [3] Ibid. pp. 142 ff.

is nothing to mark off Columba's miracles of power[1] from those of Boniface in Germany[2] or Nikon Metanoeite in the Peloponnese.[3] From Kent to Kiev mass baptism was the rule, and Vladimir's ostentatious renunciation of his people's gods[4] has the same character as that of the Northumbrian high priest Coifi more than three and a half centuries before.[5]

Yet within this over-all uniformity there is considerable diversity and, in particular, marked differences between the activities of the Greek and Latin Churches. Whatever the contribution of individuals like Nikon within the imperial frontiers,[6] the Byzantine missions, from their beginnings in the fourth century, give a general impression of organization and realistic planning, with secular and spiritual considerations frequently going hand in hand. The Cappadocian Ulfila[7] (c. 311–83) was born amongst the Goths and spoke their language. He spent much of his youth at Constantinople, was consecrated bishop there by Eusebius in c. 341 and despatched to work amongst the Goths at first beyond, and later within, the boundaries of the Empire. To assist his mission he translated the Bible into Gothic—apart from the Book of Kings, which he thought might be bad for so warlike a people. The success and importance of his mission has recently been questioned, and one commentator has gone so far as to declare that 'The Apostle of the Goths did not convert the Goths to Christianity'.[8] Though the evidence for this view is impressive, however, the judgement is in my view mistaken. The weighing of the silence of Auxentius and the comments of Ambrose against the apparently rapid conversion of the Goths once settled in Moesia, their re-

---

[1] *Adomnan's Life of St Columba*, ed. A. O. Anderson and M. O. Anderson (London 1961).

[2] *Vita S. Bonifacii*, ed. J. P. Migne, *Polattogiae Cursus Completus, Series Latina*, LXXXIX, cols. 603–34.

[3] *Vita S. Niconis*, ed. E. Martene and U. Durand, *Veterum Scriptorum et Monumentorum Historicorum, Dogmaticorum, Moralium Amplissima Collectio* (9 vols. Paris 1729), VI, cols. 837–86.

[4] *The Russian Primary Chronicle*, trans. and ed. S. H. Cross and O. P. Sherbowitz-Wetzor (Cambridge, Mass., 1953).

[5] Bede, *HE*, II, 13.

[6] See W. H. C. Frend, 'The Winning of the Countryside', *JEH*, XVIII (1967), 1–14.

[7] See E. A. Thompson, *The Visigoths in the time of Ulfila* (Oxford 1966).

[8] Ibid. p. 93.

sistance to persecution, the careers of native Goths like St Saba, and the reaction of their neighbours to them, is not by itself able either to establish or to deny Ulfila's claim to greatness. It is only when the Gothic mission is set in the wider context of the missions to the barbarians, is compared with the Irish, Pictish, or English missions that such an assessment can be made, and Ulfila be seen to have as secure a place in this evangelical movement as Patrick, Columba, or Augustine.

Byzantine missionary activity did not end with the Goths. In 543 both Justinian and Theodora sent missions to the Nubians. From the sixth century attention was concentrated on the Turkish tribes and on the remnants of the Huns near the Bosphorus, and bishoprics were established in the Crimea.[1] In the ninth century the establishment of the Norsemen at Kiev and their attack on Byzantium in 860 stimulated renewed Byzantine activity in this area. The Khazar embassy, of which Constantine-Cyril (826–69) and Methodius (c. 815–85) were important members, was the immediate Byzantine response, but Photius concentrated his efforts on evangelization, and in 866 the patriarch could claim the first short-lived conversion of the Kiev Russians.[2] Cyril and Methodius, however, had already been transferred to the north-western frontiers of the Empire, and had entered on those labours which were to give them their place in history.[3] In 862, in response to an alliance between Louis the German and the Bulgars, Ratislav, the ruler of Moravia, proposed a military and cultural alliance to the Emperor Michael III. The proposal was accepted, and two years later the Byzantine forces checked and destroyed a Bulgarian move against Moravia. The cultural results, however, were to be quite as important as the military, and at the head of the special mission despatched from Byzantium were the brothers Cyril and Methodius. They were well chosen for their task. Born and brought up in Thessalonika, they had been in close contact with the Slavs in their youth, and spoke their language. Studying subsequently at Byzantium, they had played a distinguished part

[1] Dvornik, *Making of Central...Europe*, p. 149.
[2] Ibid. pp. 65–6.
[3] For what follows, see particularly Dvornik, *Making of Central...Europe*, pp. 16–19.

2-2

in the ninth-century Byzantine cultural renaissance, and had been employed on patriarchal and imperial business. Now at the head of the Moravian mission they were to found a Slavonic Church following the Roman rite and, having invented a special alphabet, *Glagolitsa*,[1] in order to do so, to equip it with a vernacular liturgy and vernacular scriptures. Their achievement was remarkable, and though both the Moravian State and Church were to be eclipsed by the alliance of German and Magyar at the end of the ninth century, their work was not wholly destroyed. Their influence was felt in Poland; the Slavonic liturgy survived in Dalmatia and, adapted in Bulgaria to the eastern use, was transmitted to the churches of Serbia and Russia.

At Kiev, as in Moravia, the acceptance of Christianity seems to have resulted from a military alliance, whatever picturesque stories the *Russian Primary Chronicle* may record.[2] Under the terms of the treaty of 971 Vladimir had assisted the Emperor Basil II in putting down the revolt of Bardas Phocas. In return he had been promised the emperor's sister as his bride, but with the revolt past Basil was understandably reluctant to countenance the marriage of a Byzantine princess to a pagan chieftain who already had, it was reported, five wives and eight hundred concubines. It took Vladimir's capture of Kherson in 989 to bring about his marriage and conversion, and the subsequent displays of Christian piety and mass baptism at Kiev which the *Chronicle* records. 'If it were not good, the Prince and his boyars would not have accepted it,'[3] the people of Kiev are said to have exclaimed as they made their enthusiastic way into the Dnieper, but there is little indication that the conversion of Vladimir and his subjects resulted from the simple acceptance of Christian truth. In all these missionary endeavours, in fact, from the fourth to the tenth century the complexity and sophistication of Byzantine policies is evident, and there is a professional approach to evangelization which is wholly lacking in the early missions in the West, not simply in the largely individual enterprises of men like Patrick or Columba, but even

[1] Replaced in the tenth century by *Cyrilitsa*, ibid. p. 17.
[2] Ibid. pp. 169–73.
[3] *The Russian Primary Chronicle*, ed. Cross and Sherbowitz-Wetzor, p. 117.

in such an apparently organized expedition as that of Augustine in 597.

The mission which Gregory the Great sent to England had been in his mind for some time. Before he became Pope he had been frustrated in his own attempt to evangelize the 'angelic' English, and his purchase of Anglian slaves in Gaul, some time before 597, in order to educate them for the service of God in their own country was as unsuccessful as Willibrord's similar attempt at the training of young Danes a century later. The mission which Gregory finally sent was led by Augustine, who seems to have been singularly ill prepared for English conditions, and ill equipped to cope with the problems of the mission-field. Bede records that he almost abandoned 'so dangerous, arduous, and uncertain a journey'[1] right at the start; the questions he sent to Gregory from England betray a remarkable lack of initiative, and he failed to come to any arrangement with the British Church, aggravating rather than easing the situation. It is difficult, however, to lay too much of the blame on Augustine. He was Gregory's choice, and it was Gregory with his grandiose schemes of diocesan organization who showed himself totally out of touch with the position of the infant Church in England. Such ignorance was to continue. In 668, when the English Church was leaderless, very nearly bishopless, ravaged by plague, and threatened with widespread apostasy, the Pope sought a new Archbishop of Canterbury. Hadrian, the first choice, refused and 'proposed to the Pope the monk Andrew...chaplain to a neighbouring convent of women and...considered worthy of a bishopric by all who knew him'.[2] It was a fortunate chance which sent Theodore of Tarsus to Canterbury, but even then he was allowed to delay in Rome for a further four months, allowing his hair to grow, so that he could be correctly tonsured. There seems to have been singularly little realization of English problems at Rome at this period.

Perhaps the most remarkable limitation of the Augustinian mission, however, was its inability to speak the language of those to whom it was sent. The monks were, Bede records, 'appalled at the idea of going to a barbarous, fierce, and pagan nation, of whose

[1] Bede, *HE*, I, 23.   [2] Ibid. IV, I.

very language they were ignorant',[1] and Gregory ordered them to obtain interpreters from among the Franks.

Nor was it simply a matter of learning English. As late as the fourteenth century John of Trevisa commented 'It seemeth a great wonder how English, that is the birth tongue of Englishmen, and their own language and tongue, is so diverse of sound in this one island...'and later remarked 'All the language of the Northumbrians, and specially at York, is so sharp, slitting, frotting, and unshape that we southern men may that language never understand'.[2] A century later Caxton's Kentish housewife assured herself of lasting fame when, asked by a fellow-countryman for *egges*, she replied that she knew no French, and only understood the question when asked for *eyren*. In Italy, Dante remarked that there were more than a thousand varieties of Italian vernacular in his day, while as late as *c.* 1515 Machiavelli could state that there was no language which could be called the common tongue of the country.[3] In twelfth-century France Abelard, born in the Romance-speaking border territory south-east of Nantes, found that as abbot of St Gildas, south of Vannes, he could not understand the Celtic dialect spoken there by his fellow Bretons.[4]

Such variations and differences added to the difficulties which faced the missionary, and Augustine was not unique in encountering them. Agilbert, Birinus's Frankish successor in Wessex, offered to evangelize the kingdom in spite of knowing no English, and was accepted by the king as 'chief bishop'. 'Later, however, the king, who understood only Saxon, grew tired of the bishop's foreign speech, and invited to the province a bishop of his own race...'[5] At Whitby, Agilbert, as the senior representative of Roman views, was asked to speak in the Roman cause. Instead, he nominated Wilfrid, since he could 'explain our position in the English language more competently than I can do through an interpreter'.[6] It is difficult to believe that Felix, a Burgundian, in

[1] Ibid. I, 23.
[2] John of Trevisa, *Descrypcion of Englonde*.
[3] All quoted by M. Aston, *The Fifteenth Century* (London 1968), pp. 40–2.
[4] M. M. McLaughlin, 'Abelard as Autobiographer: the Motives and Meaning of his "Story of Calamities"', *Speculum*, XLII (1967), 463–88.
[5] Bede, *HE*, III, 7.   [6] Ibid. III, 25.

The shadow of the Christian symbol

East Anglia, Birinus in Wessex, or Hadrian and Theodore on their arrival in England, can have been in any better position.

At an earlier date, Columba's mission to King Brude near Inverness had been accompanied by native interpreters,[1] and in spite of the fact that he had been studying the language since his arrival at Iona two years before Columba still preached to Patrick's 'apostate Picts'[2] through these intermediaries. In early seventh-century Northumbria King Oswald himself interpreted for Aidan on his early missions until the saint learnt the language.[3] In the tenth century Adalbert of Prague attempted to address the pagan Prussians in Polish, then closely akin to his native Czech.[4] In the eleventh, the megalomaniac Archbishop of Hamburg–Bremen, Adalbert, was put firmly in his place by the Danish king, who told him 'that the barbarian peoples could more easily be converted by men like them in language and custom than by persons un-acquainted with their ways and strange to their kind'.[5] In the early thirteenth century the first Franciscan mission to Germany came to an ignominious end when the friars discovered that their scant German—the single word *Ja* in answer to all questions—not only obtained food and lodging for them, but also branded them as dangerous heretics.[6]

Whatever the impact allowed to the interpreted appeal of the evangelist—and Columba seems to have converted an entire family in this way—and however readily it is accepted, as with Bernardino of Siena, that the missionary message was communicated more by the dramatic force of the occasion than by actual comprehension of the evangelist's words, it is still difficult to avoid adverse

[1] *Adomnan*, II, 32.

[2] *Epistola ad christianos Corotici tyranni subditos*, ed. J. P. Migne, *Patrologia Latina* (Paris 1865), LIII, col. 817, VIII.

[3] Bede, *HE*, III, 3: And while the bishop, who was not yet fluent in the English language, preached the Gospel, it was most delightful to see the king himself interpreting the word of God to his thegns and leaders, for he himself had obtained perfect command of the Scottish tongue during his long exile.

[4] Dvornik, *Making of Central...Europe*, p. 132.

[5] Adam of Bremen, *The History of the Archbishops of Hamburg–Bremen*, ed. F. J. Tschan (Columbia 1959), III, lxxii.

[6] Jordan of Giano, trans. G. G. Coulton, *Social Life in Britain from the Conquest to the Reformation* (Cambridge 1918).

comparison between Western missions and those emanating from the Byzantine world, with their sound groundwork and preparation, and it is a comparison which is not limited simply to the spoken word. There was, for example, no Anglo-Saxon Bible or liturgy produced by Augustine or his successors, and nearly three centuries later Alfred 'wondered exceedingly at those good and wise men who were in former times throughout England, and had fully studied all those books, that they would not turn any part of them into their own language';[1] unlike Goths, Copts, Nubians, and Slavs, the English had to learn Latin.

All these circumstances tended to reinforce the natural and political tendency of the missionary to seek out and convert the local ruler. In discussions at that level it was probably less important than we might imagine to be able to speak the regional language, and once the ruler was won over, the rest would follow. In Kent, Northumbria, Moravia, Russia, everywhere the same pattern is apparent. Convert the prince, and an enforced or sycophantic general acceptance of Christianity resulted. Ethelbert of Kent 'would not compel anyone to accept Christianity, for he had learned from his instructors...that the service of Christ must be accepted freely, and not under compulsion; nevertheless he showed greater favour to believers'.[2] Vladimir of Kiev proclaimed that 'if any inhabitant, rich or poor, did not betake himself to the river Dnieper, he would risk the Prince's displeasure'.[3] It was during Ethelbert's supremacy that the Roman mission extended its influence to Essex and East Anglia, and at a later period Boniface and Willibrord owed much of their success to Frankish protection. The coin had its reverse side, however. The Roman mission in Northumbria was eclipsed with the defeat and death of Edwin; there was a pagan reaction in Essex and Kent on the death of Saberht and Ethelred, and the first conversion of the Kiev Russians was nullified when Askold was slain by Oleg of Novgorod.[4] The spread of the faith could be hindered, too, by its association with

[1] *Pastoral Care*, prose preface, trans. D. Whitelock, *EHD* (London 1955), I, 818–19.
[2] Bede, *HE*, I, 26.
[3] *The Russian Primary Chronicle*, ed. Cross and Sherbowitz-Wetzor, p. 117.
[4] Dvornik, *Making of Central...Europe*, pp. 65–6.

political policies. The antagonism between Goths and Romans imposed a slow start on the Gothic mission. Columba's move to Iona may well have been due to his involvement in the dynastic feuds which led to the battle of Culdreihme (561). For the slaughter there the local churches held him responsible, and for a time he was excommunicate. Boniface was martyred as soon as he ventured beyond the shield of Frankish power into non-Frankish Frisia. For the Polabian Slavs 'the Christian God was no other than the German God',[1] and Adalbert suffered as much from Prussian hostility to Polish policies as from antagonism to the Christian message that he brought.[2] Indeed, when the composite character of the Christian message that was preached is examined, it becomes difficult to see what opposition could have been aroused to it, except from the vested interests of priestly or bardic castes, for the Church was seeking to incorporate much that was pagan into the Christian life.

Gregory the Great outlines the policy in advice which he gave to Augustine:

We have been giving careful thought to the affairs of the English, and have come to the conclusion that the temples of the idols in that country should on no account be destroyed. You are to destroy the idols, but the temples themselves are to be aspersed with holy water, altars are to be set up, and relics enclosed in them...

In this way, we hope that the people, seeing that its temples are not destroyed, may abandon idolatry, and resort to those places as before...And since they have a custom of sacrificing many oxen to devils, let some other solemnity be substituted in its place, such as a day of Dedication...They are no longer to sacrifice beasts to the Devil, but they may kill them for food to the praise of God.[3]

One is reminded of Theodoret of Cyrrhus's comment that in fifth-century Syria 'instead of the former disgraceful orgies there were decorous and orderly celebrations'.[4] Decorous and orderly they may have been, but the important point is that they were celebrations, and on the same occasions and in the same places as 'the former disgraceful orgies'. Examples could be multiplied—it was

[1] Ibid. p. 129. [2] Ibid. pp. 131–5.
[3] Bede, *HE*, I, 30. [4] Quoted Frend, 'Winning of the Countryside', p. 4.

no accident that the oak-topped hills of Ireland favoured by the druids should similarly attract Christian settlement, and at Derry Columba built the church off the east–west axis to avoid chopping down the trees. It is not difficult to see a similarity between Agilbert's appointment as 'chief bishop' in Wessex and the *primus pontificum* of the Northumbrians or the *princeps sacerdotum* of the South Saxons.[1] But the position may be summed up in Bruno of Querfurt's comment on Adalbert's mission to the Hungarians: 'Adalbert also visited them personally, and when they had forsaken some of their errors he raised over them the shadow of the Christian symbol.'[2]

It can indeed be doubted whether the majority of these countryfolk were Christian at all, except in name. An earlier paper to this society[3] stressed the tenacity of paganism in an apparently Christian empire, and evidence of a later date indicates that it did not die easily. The Council of Narbonne, held in 589, was horrified to learn that many Catholics kept Thursday as a holiday because it was Thor's day.[4] Boniface, in a letter to Pope Zacharias on his accession to the papacy in 742, complained of the continuance of pagan customs, not merely in Rome, but at St Peter's itself, and the Pope's reply admitted the justice of the accusation.[5] Adalbert's first exile from his see at Prague was ascribed to the continuing strength of the pagan opposition in Bohemia; his return was marred for him when he found the sabbath being broken by a rowdy market-day at Pilsen,[6] and his second exile, whatever the politics behind it, was occasioned by the execution of the pagan death-penalty for adultery upon a woman to whom he had given sanctuary.[7]

It was, however, perhaps the corruption of Christians by pagan practice rather than the continuing paganism within Christendom

[1] See Thompson, *Visigoths in the time of Ulfila*, p. 58 n. 1.
[2] Dvornik, *Making of Central...Europe*, pp. 133–4, 152.
[3] Frend, 'Winning of the Countryside'.
[4] Thompson, *Visigoths in the time of Ulfila*, p. 92.
[5] C. H. Talbot, *The Anglo-Saxon Missionaries in Germany* (London 1954), Ep. 27, 28 (M. Tangl, *Die Briefe des Heiligen Bonifatius*, Ep. 50, 51).
[6] Dvornik, *Making of Central...Europe*, p. 113.
[7] Ibid. pp. 113–14.

which menaced the faith more. Popes and saints might inveigh against the black arts and recourse to sorcerers, but there is little difference between pagan acceptance of the supernatural and magical, and Christian of the often rather sordidly miraculous. Pagan magic had to be countered by Christian, as Columba demonstrated in his contest with the Pictish magician Broichan,[1] and when the Christian God seemed to fail, men returned to the old ways, to those 'false remedies of idolatry' which Cuthbert had denounced,[2] and to those altars which Theodore of Tarsus found being refurbished when he arrived in England in time of plague. Christianity had, in fact, been established on the same footing as the cults that it sought to displace, and there must have been many who could have said, with Augustine of Hippo's famous parishioner, 'To be sure I visit the idols, I consult magicians and soothsayers, but I do not forsake the church of God. I am a Catholic'.[3]

It is this which makes it unreal to talk in terms either of large-scale conversion or of widespread apostasy at this period, and on that basis to assert or to deny the missionary claims of a man like Ulfila. From fourth-century Italy to tenth-century Yorkshire or Normandy the daily life, the religious and social attitudes, of the *pagani* were largely unaffected by the essential principles of the Christian faith. A Christian paganism had been established, and as the later medieval domestic missions, and the sixteenth-century Cornish peasants who rose in defence of their 'Christmas games' in 1549 showed, it was to have a long life. Christianity was not to be established by spectacular conversions, diplomatic treaties, or the elaboration of large schemes of ecclesiastical organization. It could only be created by individual example at the grass-roots— St Anthony, knowing no Greek, but able to preach the simple message of the Gospel in the vernacular;[4] Martin of Tours, who 'possessed all the dignity proper to a bishop without deserting the way of life and the virtue of a monk'.[5] Priests were few and far

---

[1] *Adomnan*, II, 33, 34.   [2] Bede, *HE*, IV, 27.
[3] Quoted Frend, 'Winning of the Countryside', p. 8.
[4] 'The Scriptures are enough for instruction', Athanasius, *Vita Antonii*, 16.
[5] Sidonius Apollinarius, *Epistolae*, IX. See 'Saint Martin et son temps', *Studia Anselmiana*, XLVI (1961), 6.

between, whether in Colman's Northumbria[1] or Boniface's Wessex,[2] and it was to Cuthbert that the Northumbrian peasants complained that 'men had robbed them of their old ways of worship, and there were none who knew how the new ways should be conducted'.[3] What was needed was an Aidan to dispense first 'the milk of simple teaching' to 'an uncivilized people of an obstinate and barbarous temperament', and then proceed to 'greater perfection',[4] or a Cuthbert

to visit and preach in the villages that lay far distant among high and inaccessible mountains, which others feared to visit, and where barbarity and squalor daunted other teachers...it would sometimes be a week, sometimes two or three, and occasionally an entire month before he returned home, remaining in the mountains to guide the peasants heavenwards by his teachings and virtuous example.[5]

Europe may have seemed Christian in the year 1000, but it was only 'the shadow of the Christian symbol' which had been cast. The real conversion remained to be achieved, and the propagation of the faith would have been better served if the Church had not become preoccupied with reconciling Greek subtleties, Roman systems, or pagan customs to the faith, and had borne in mind Columbanus's precept, 'He who says he believes in Christ ought to walk as Christ walked, poor and humble and always preaching truth'.[6]

[1] Bede, *HE*, III, 26: When a priest visited a village, the people were quick to gather in some cottage to hear the word of life, for priests and clerics always came to a village solely to preach, baptize, visit the sick, and, in short, to care for the souls of its people.

[2] Willibald, *Vita S. Bonifacii*, ed. J. P. Migne, *Patrologia Latina* (Paris 1863), LXXXIX, col. 605, 3: 'Cum vero aliqui, sicut illis regionibus moris est, presbyteri sive clerici, populares vel laicos praedicandi causa adissent, et ad villam domumque praefati patrisfamilias venissent...'

[3] Quoted P. H. Blair, *Roman Britain and Early England* (London 1963), p. 232.

[4] Bede, *HE*, III, 5.

[5] Bede, *HE*, IV, 27.

[6] *Sancti Columbani Opera*, ed. G. S. M. Walker (Dublin 1957).

GREGORY THE GREAT AND A PAPAL MISSIONARY STRATEGY

by R. A. MARKUS

I N his *Ecclesiastical History of the English People* Bede includes[1] a deservedly famous letter[2] of Gregory I containing the Pope's instructions to his missionaries in Kent on how to go about converting the heathen English to Christianity. The letter is addressed to Abbot Mellitus, one of the band of reinforcements sent to England from Rome in June 601. In it Mellitus is asked to instruct Augustine, established at Canterbury for the last four years, that 'the sanctuaries of the idols among this nation should on no account be destroyed'; by all means, let the idols go; but the temples, if they be soundly constructed, need only be sprinkled with holy water and consecrated to the worship of the true God. In this way hardened English minds may be won to a stepwise ascent and not be required to make too large a leap of faith.

It is too easy to see in this letter no more than Gregory's characteristic good sense, moderation, and tact. That it is evidence of these traits of his mind, we need not doubt. But that it is also much more than this has not, so far as I know, been noticed.[3] English scholarship has perhaps been somewhat spoiled by having so superb a historian as Bede for its main primary source in this period. It is worth, on occasion, to take Gregorian material out of its context in Bede, and to consider it in relation to its papal, Roman context. This process may serve—and I hope to show that it does, in this instance, serve—to throw Bede's qualities as a historian into even sharper relief.

---

[1] *HE*, I, 30.
[2] *Epist.* XI, 56. References to Gregory's correspondence are in the edition by Ewald and Hartmann, *MGH, Epist.* I and II.
[3] Except for a hint in my paper, 'The chronology of the Gregorian mission to England: Bede's narrative and Gregory's correspondence', *JEH*, XIV (1963), 23 n. 2.

The English mission was certainly one of Gregory's most momentous initiatives; Erich Caspar has seen it as the crowning and most personal of his works, on which his claim to greatness primarily rests.[1] It was not, however, Gregory's only interest in missionary activity, nor was it the first time he indulged his taste for it. Within four months of his accession to the papacy he was writing[2] to the Italian bishops to encourage them to preach the Catholic faith unremittingly among the Arian subjects of the Lombard king; and preaching the Gospel to heretics, Jews, and pagans remained a continuous though thin thread discernible among the manifold concerns of his pontificate. There is, however, a good deal of uncertainty about how Gregory expected the Gospel to be preached, and a good deal of variety in his instructions. Among the Lombards, the 'unspeakable' King Authari[3] had prohibited the administration of Catholic baptism among his subjects in 590. Preaching was now the only feasible hope of reconciling Arians to Catholicism; nothing else could be done in the situation, and this is what the Pope prescribed. But preaching the Gospel takes a less pure form in some of the other 'missions', if we may call them such, in which Gregory at one time or another interested himself.

The Jews always formed a special category in Gregory's dealings with non-Christians. In the scrupulous concern for justice and humanity Gregory's attitude to the Jews[4] contrasts starkly with the measures taken against them at much the same time in Visigothic Spain. It was in a letter[5] he wrote to an Italian bishop, reprimanding him for hounding out the local Jewish community from its successive places of worship, that Gregory laid down the principle that 'those who do not agree with the Christian religion should be brought to the unity of faith by mildness and generosity, by admonition and persuasion; otherwise men who might be won to believing by the sweetness of preaching and the fear of the coming judgement will be repulsed by threats and pressure'. This was his settled principle when dealing with Jews. He was

---

[1] *Geschichte des Papsttums*, II (Tübingen 1933), 506.
[2] *Epist.* I, 17; cf. II, 4.   [3] *Epist.* I, 17.
[4] E.g. *Epist.* I, 42; VIII, 25; IX, 38, 40, 195; XIII, 15.
[5] *Epist.* I, 34; cf. II, 6.

certainly not squeamish about reinforcing preaching with a little extraneous aid. Conversion was to be made easy, even profitable.[1] If you really wish to convert people to the true faith, he once wrote with engaging frankness, you should seek to do it with the aid of a little blandishment (*blandimentis*) rather than by harsh threats (*asperitatibus*).[2] The blandishment could take as advantageous a form as a remission of rent conceded to Jewish peasants on Church lands if they became converts to Christianity.[3] So far as the Jews are concerned, Gregory's missionary policy may be summarized in his own words:[4] by preaching, not by force. Although 'preaching' is certainly to be understood as seasoned with a little 'blandishment', there is no trace of support for coercion.[5]

This was not, however, Gregory's view on how to convert the heathen (and Manichees, who tend to be reckoned with them) to Christianity. Apart from the English, Gregory knew of heathens in Sicily, in Sardinia, and in Corsica, and he cared about their salvation. In Sicily, the *praetor* at the head of the civil administration was asked to help in seeking out and punishing heathens and Manichees;[6] the agent in charge of the Roman Church's lands in Sicily was told to devote his energy to 'persecuting zealously the Manichees on our lands, and to recall them to the Catholic faith';[7] one of his successors in the job, apparently more zealous in persecuting the *incantatores atque sortilegos*, was commended for his zeal, and mildly rebuked for thinking that his zeal would not be pleasing to the Pope.[8]

Little is known about the situation in Corsica at this time.[9] In Sardinia there is clear evidence of well-established pockets of

---

[1] Cf. *Epist.* II, 38; VI, 29; VIII, 23. [2] *Epist.* XIII, 15.
[3] *Epist.* V, 7. [4] *Epist.* I, 45.
[5] The congratulations which Gregory offered to King Reccared on his anti-Semitic legislation are altogether out of keeping with the prevailing mood of his instructions to the Italian bishops and agents on Church lands. His warm approval of the Visigothic measures I think refers only to their attempt to extirpate Christian slavery to Jewish masters. His correspondence abounds with censures of repeated instances of this, and he seems to have been particularly worried about the prevalence of this abuse in Visigothic Narbonne. This might explain his apparent inconsistency.
[6] *Epist.* III, 59. [7] *Epist.* V, 7.
[8] *Epist.* XI, 33. [9] *Epist.* VIII, 1.

heathenism in the north, and the see of Fausiana was revived to serve as a missionary base to cope with it.[1] How important a role its preaching and ministry were expected to play in converting the pagan Barbaricini of Sardinia it is impossible to say. It is clear, however, that the Pope envisaged other measures as well from the start. Landowners were admonished to bring their peasants to the worship of the true God;[2] peasants reluctant 'to come to God' were to be 'so burdened with rent that the weight of this punitive exaction should make them hasten to righteousness';[3] bishops were threatened with severe penalties if any pagan peasants were found on their estates.[4] Local military commanders were praised for their efforts in bringing pagans to the service of Christ and exhorted to persevere in them,[5] and the local governor was asked to help in converting the heathen.[6] Less realistically, a pagan chieftain who had, apparently alone among his tribe, become a Christian, was exhorted to bring all he could from his tribe to faith in Christ.[7] Even so, Gregory had occasion to complain at the imperial court that the authorities in Sardinia allowed bribes to make them too compliant with pagan worship.[8] What was it that these local officials, allegedly bribed, were accused of neglecting? The clue is given in another letter where the measures against the heathen are specified: those who will not listen to reason, if they are slaves, 'are to be chastised by beating and torture, whereby they might be brought to amendment'; free men are to be jailed.[9]

If Gregory had conceived a 'missionary strategy' for Augustine's mission to England, it was one dominated by thoughts like these about the Sardinian missions of 594, two years before Augustine was despatched. So far as one can tell from the evidence of his letters, Gregory knew next to nothing about the English kingdoms, about the political geography—except as it had been in Roman times—or about the religious situation in Britain at the time he sent off the first missionaries in 596. By 601, however, the

---

[1] *Epist.* IV, 29.   [2] *Epist.* IV, 23.
[3] *Epist.* IV, 26.   [4] Ibid.
[5] *Epist.* IV, 25.   [6] *Epist.* XI, 12.
[7] *Epist.* IV, 27.   [8] *Epist.* V, 38.
[9] *Epist.* IX, 204.

first reports on the state of affairs in England were beginning to come in. In the late spring of that year Augustine's representatives were on their way to get reinforcements from Rome; and there they had arrived by June. With their requests they brought information which helped the Pope to fill in the blanks in his picture. In June 601 the band of missionaries sent to help Augustine were setting off, armed with a great batch of letters, to all and sundry either actually concerned with the mission, or near the route their bearers were to take. Among these letters there are four in which the Pope gives us a glimpse into his thoughts about the policy of the mission. There were two letters to Augustine: in one,[1] the Pope outlined his well-known plan for the division of the island, on the lines of the Roman administrative geography but without any relation to the political actualities of the sixth or seventh centuries, into ecclesiastical provinces and dioceses. In the other,[2] Augustine was admonished only on one single point: we must give thanks to God for the 'exterior miracles' by which it has pleased God to draw the English 'to interior grace'; and Augustine must guard against being elated by success and preserve his humility in the midst of thaumaturgy. Apart from Augustine's miracles, it was the support of the king to the preaching of the Gospel on which Gregory laid most weight.

It is in his letters addressed to King Aethelberht[3] and to Queen Bertha[4] that we get closest to Gregory's mind on this question.[5] The queen is admonished 'to strengthen the mind of [her] glorious husband in the love of the Christian faith', to 'kindle his concern for the fullest conversion of the people subject to his rule'; and the king is bidden to 'guard with a zealous mind the divinely given grace [he] has received, to hasten to spread the Christian faith among the peoples subject to [him]...to repress the worship of idols, to destroy the shrines, to raise the morals of [his] subjects by the example of [his] own purity of life, by admonition and warning, by rewarding and punishing'.

[1] *Epist.* XI, 39 = *HE*, I, 29. [2] *Epist.* XI, 36 = (in part) *HE*, I, 31.
[3] *Epist.* XI, 37 = *HE*, I, 32. [4] *Epist.* XI, 35.
[5] I have discussed the interpretation of these letters in my paper referred to above, p. 29 n. 3.

The example of Constantine was held up to him, of the emperor who 'subjected the Roman Empire along with himself to Almighty God and our Lord Jesus Christ'; and as the Pope had some inkling that Aethelberht was something more than a mere king of Kent, he asked him to do his utmost 'to bring the knowledge of the one God, Father, Son and Holy Spirit, to the kings and peoples subject to [him]'. The awareness of Aethelberht's influence beyond the borders of Kent and the magnificence with which the imperial model invests the king are the only things which distinguish Gregory's expectations of the English king from his expectations of a minor chieftain in Sardinia,[1] recently converted, like Aethelberht, to Christianity. The strategy of the English mission was conceived along a straight line running continuously through Gregory's missions among the heathen elsewhere. Coercion by the available authorities was an unquestioned prop of the Gospel, and the prototype was ready to hand in the image of Constantine and the establishment of the Christian Roman Empire.

The policy outlined in the letter to Mellitus[2] does not fit easily into this picture. The instruction that the 'shrines of the idols should on no account be destroyed' (*fana idolorum...minime destrui debeant*) reads like a direct contradiction of the instructions given to the king: 'destroy the shrines' (*fanorum aedificia everte*), and the tenor of the whole letter is very different. Instead of enforcing Christianity through royal power and influence, all the stress is here laid on accommodating the preaching of the Gospel to hardened English hearts. The Pope is, of course, writing to a bishop in one case, a king in the other; but it is hard to see how the bishop could be categorically told 'on no account to destroy' what the king was expected to destroy. The difference in recipients will not account for the discrepancy between the policies laid down in the two letters. The letter to Mellitus taken as a whole reads like a clear and deliberate countermanding of the instructions to Aethelberht.

This is precisely what it is. The fact has often been concealed from scholarly English eyes on account of their—quite under-

---

[1] Cf. *Epist.* IV, 27, referred to above.
[2] *Epist.* XI, 56 = *HE*, I, 30, referred to on p. 29, above.

standable—habit of looking at the letter solely in the context given it by Bede. Not only does its place in Gregory's over-all missionary policies, naturally, not appear in this context; but even its chronological relation to the other Bedan letters, and particularly to the letter to Aethelberht, is left obscure. In fact, the letter to Mellitus was written almost exactly a month after the letter to the king: 18 July and 22 June respectively. It was sent to Mellitus after his departure from Rome, *en route* for England, before any news had reached the Pope about his journey. In the papal register it bears the title 'To Abbot Mellitus in the Frankish lands' (*in Franciis*); and its position in our collections of Gregorian letters—followed by Ewald and Hartmann in their definitive reconstruction of the Register—indicates clearly that it belongs to the letters sent out late in July. The learned Plummer, even though he did not have Hartmann's edition of the letters at his disposal, did in fact adopt the correct date, though with a query. But even he did not notice the curious contradictions between Gregory's two sets of instructions, separated by only a month.

The reason for the discrepancy between the two letters becomes plain as soon as one places them in their proper Gregorian context. We need only visualize the Pope in June 601, up to now almost entirely ignorant of conditions in Britain, receiving Augustine's messengers in Rome. Overjoyed by their reports of his success, he despatches a further band of missionaries under Abbot Mellitus's command. At the same time, he has heard about the slow headway the mission is making in England; perhaps the king has not put his weight behind its work as much as a king should? At any rate, a little exhortation to this end can do no harm, and Gregory had a whole pile of precedents in his own correspondence for writing to him in the vein he now adopted. The first thought to come into his mind was to apply, once again, the customary missionary methods deployed on previous occasions, the mission backed by coercive power. With their brief framed in these terms, Mellitus and his men depart, with every appearance of haste, within the month. There is a quality of breathless haste in the accumulation of letters on 22 June: everybody who needs a letter who has not yet been written to in the course of the preceding days is now quickly written to: the Frankish and English output of the papal writing office rises to a great climax on 22 June, as if the writing office were frantically working to a suddenly imposed deadline, and then abruptly stops. The whole body of this material suggests to me a very rapid turn-round—the messengers' arrival about the beginning of June; their departure very soon after 22 June, bearing the Pope's letters with them. How little the first reports about Britain had done to produce a realistic appraisal of the situation by the Pope may be gauged from the provisions he made for the establishment of ecclesiastical provinces and dioceses: no more information was required for these than could be gained from an administrative map of Roman Britain. The Pope had little information, and the little took some time to sink in. Did he perceive its implications as soon as Mellitus was gone? Gregory took pause to think, and he had second thoughts: perhaps he had not quite understood the reports about the king's reluctance; perhaps his admonitions to the king had been somewhat unrealistic? If such were his thoughts—and we can only conjecture this—they were undoubtedly right. We know, as Bede knew, the entrenched strength of English paganism which forced the Kentish king to proceed with tact and caution and prevented him from taking the path of coercion;[1] we know, as Bede knew, the tenacity of the old religion shown in its resurgence in Kent and Essex on the death of King Aethelberht.[2] It is not impossible that in the weeks after Mellitus's departure the realities of this situation gradually dawned on Gregory. He had after all, as he himself says in his letter, 'thought long and deeply' (*diu mecum cogitans tractavi*) on the matter. And if my conjecture is the right reconstruction of his thought during that month, then we need not be surprised by his change of mind and his urgent, dramatic despatch[3] of the letter containing his second thoughts to Mellitus, now on his way, somewhere in Gaul.

[1] Cf. *HE*, I, 26. [2] Cf. *HE*, II, 5–6.

[3] Gregory's usual procedure is to make maximum use of any available messenger. Unlike all the remaining correspondence with England and Gaul, this letter appears to have been despatched by itself through a special messenger.

Here was a real turning point in the development of papal missionary strategy. The settled, almost unquestioned policy of reliance on coercion by the secular authorities suddenly, under the pressure and the demands of a new situation, gave way to quite another conception. More than a century later, writing within a milieu in which Bede's work was well known, Bishop Daniel of Winchester gave advice to Boniface, then labouring among the Germans: argue with them, he said, 'without insulting or irritating them, but gently and with great tact'.[1] Here was a man who, though remote from the missionary situation, had learnt the lesson which the consciousness of a new situation had forced upon Gregory.

I should like, in conclusion, to suggest that Bede may well have been conscious of the significance of Gregory's letter to Mellitus. The dating clause of the letter in the manuscripts of the *Ecclesiastical History* is in fact a tangle. While we are awaiting Sir Roger Mynors's edition, it may suffice to note that a number of manuscripts, including two of the most important early texts, the Moore and the Leningrad manuscripts, omit the month from the dating clause altogether, and close the gap so as to produce nonsense. It is certainly curious that two of the best early and independent witnesses to the text should do this; and the fact suggests that Bede's autograph contained a gap or an unresolved query at this point. Such a gap could be accounted for as follows: Nothelm, digging in the Lateran archives, copied all the letters which, from the marginal titles they bore in the register, appeared to be concerned with the English mission. The letter to Mellitus, though a month later than the last of the batch despatched with Mellitus, in fact occurs in the register only a few pages later (there are only four letters intervening). Thinking of it as part of the same batch, Nothelm could easily have made the slip of writing 'June' instead of 'July'. If he did, then the date as shown on his copy transmitted to Bede would make the letter precede the letter to Aethelberht by five days. Bede duly preserved the two letters in the sequence in which they came to him, and inserted the letter to Mellitus into his *History* before the letter

[1] Tangl, no. 37.

to the king. But being a more acute judge of historical circumstances, and noting the discrepancy between the two letters, he was puzzled, and decided to leave the month blank, perhaps pending further investigation. It was left for subsequent copyists to close the gap, and incidentally, in doing so, to reveal a facet of Bede's acute historical sense and meticulous care in using his material.

ST COLUMBAN: MONK OR MISSIONARY?

by the late G. S. M. WALKER

MY subject has been under discussion recently, for example by Ludwig Bieler in the 1966 Spoleto Settimane[1] and at a more popular level by Brendan Lehane in his *Quest of Three Abbots*.[2] But for me the question was raised fourteen years ago, when I was editing the Latin works of St Columban,[3] and Aubrey Gwynn showed me much kindness in correspondence. He mentioned *inter alia* the comments of Bishop Galvin, then nearing the end of his long life as a missionary to China. Galvin first went out as a young priest in 1912 to serve a mission in Hanyang. Returning on furlough in 1918, he made a celebrated appeal to the members of Maynooth College for the conversion of the Chinese, as a result of which he was joined by Father John Blowick in founding the Irish Congregation of St Columban, popularly known as the Maynooth Mission to China. Soon appointed Vicar Apostolic, Galvin later became Bishop of Hanyang, and stayed in his diocese under a series of trials, persecution, and house arrest, until he was expelled from the country in 1952. He told a friend that he would never have survived his experiences had it not been for a constant memory of Columban's example, and he felt that he had enjoyed the saint's companionship for forty years. Though not an academic scholar, Bishop Galvin is entitled by the circumstances of his life to judge the spirituality of Columban, and he criticized my original statement that his patron was 'a monk, not a missionary'. The bishop may have been reading his own vocation into that of the saint, but in deference to his views I altered my text and wrote: 'he was a missionary through circumstance, a monk by

---

[1] *La Conversione al Cristianesimo nell'Europa dell'alto Medioevo* (1967), 559–80.
[2] I.e. Brendan, Columba, Columban (1968).
[3] A new edition of *S. Columbani Opera* (Dublin 1957) is in preparation; Professor Bieler has generously undertaken the bulk of the textual revision.

vocation; a contemplative, too frequently driven to action by the vices of the world; a pilgrim, on the road to Paradise'.[1]

This verdict is, I think, justified by the evidence of Columban's own writings. Roughly one-quarter of these comprise two monastic rules and a penitential giving guidance on perfection in the spiritual life, primarily for monks but also for such lay people as submitted to his ascetic discipline. His thirteen sermons also were delivered to monks, and stress the interior virtues. Out of six letters two are addressed to monks, three to popes, and one to a Frankish synod. Finally his poems contain spiritual instruction, advising renunciation of the world,[2] and in the *De Mundi Transitu* rising to a critique of worldliness comparable to some of the great medieval hymns—

> De terrenis eleva
> Tui cordis oculos;
> Ama amantissimos
> Angelorum populos... [3]

The same note sounds in his sermons: 'this world shall pass, and daily passes and revolves towards its end... propped on pillars of vanity'.[4] But his attitude is not entirely negative. Human life on earth is not the true life, but it is a way that leads towards the life eternal—'via ergo es ad vitam, non vita; vera enim es via sed non plana, aliis longa, aliis brevis, aliis lata, aliis angusta, aliis laeta, aliis tristis, omnibus similiter festinans et irrevocabilis'.[5] Hence the purpose of life is a pilgrimage to heaven—'viatorum est festinare ad patriam... ibi enim patria ubi Pater noster est'[6]— and our sojourn on earth is that of travellers at an inn—'sic vivamus in via ut viatores, ut peregrini, ut hospites mundi'[7]— with the prospect of a blessed eternity before us—'iustorum autem vitae finis est vita aeterna, requies, pax perennis, patria caelestis, aeternitas beata, laetitia infinita'.[8] The same concept of pilgrimage appears in Columban's letters. He calls his monks

---

[1] *S. Columbani Opera*, p. xxxii.
[2] *Ad Hunaldum*, 5 (*Opera*, p. 184); *ad Sethum*, 8 (186).
[3] *De Mundi Transitu*, 89–92 (184).
[4] *Instructio*, III, 1 (72).   [5] *Instr.* v, 1 (84); cf. v, 2 (86), VI, 1 (86), IX, 1 (98).
[6] *Instr.* VIII, 1 (94).   [7] *Instr.* VIII, 2 (96).   [8] *Instr.* IX, 1 (96).

'comperegrini'[1] and says that he himself entered Gaul 'pro Christo salvatore...peregrinus'.[2]

But the pilgrim must help others forward on their journey, so that the concept of pilgrimage merges into that of mission. Hence Columban wished to visit the heathen and 'evangelium eis a nobis praedicari'.[3] His thought comes to clearest expression in the prayer[4] which closes his twelfth sermon:

Lord grant me, I pray Thee in the name of Jesus Christ Thy Son my God, that love which knows no fall, so that my lamp may feel the kindling touch and not be quenched, may burn for me and for others may give light. Do Thou, O Christ, deign to kindle our lamps, Thou Saviour most sweet to us, that they may shine continually in Thy temple and receive perpetual light from Thee the Light perpetual, so that our darkness may be enlightened and yet the world's darkness may be driven from us. Thus do Thou enrich my lantern with Thy light, I pray Thee Jesus mine, so that by its light there may be disclosed to me those holy places of the holy, which hold Thee the eternal Priest of the eternal things, entering there in the pillars of that great temple of Thine, that constantly I may see, observe, desire Thee only, and loving Thee alone may behold, and before Thee my lamp may ever shine and burn...'

The lamp in burning inevitably gives light to others, but its primary purpose is to shine amid the glories of eternity. Thus also the monk, aflame with divine fire, may assume an apostolate to others; but his chief end is still to glorify God in contemplation.

Columban's biography[5] by Jonas tells the same tale. It was the approaches of some lascivious girls that first drove the youthful saint to the cell of an Irish anchoress, who said that she had spent fifteen years in her 'peregrinationis locus' and would have gone farther afield if it had not been for the weakness of her sex.[6] After bearing Christ's yoke at Bangor under Comgall[7] for many years, Columban 'cepit peregrinationem desiderare', remembering God's word to Abraham, 'Exi de terra tua'.[8] Taking

---

[1] *Epist.* I, 8 (10).   [2] *Epist.* II, 6 (16).

[3] *Epist.* IV, 5 (30).   [4] *Instr.* XII, 3 (14).

[5] The edition by Krusch in *MGH* has now been superseded by that of M. Tosi (Piacenza 1965).   [6] *Vita Col.* I, 3 (Tosi 14).

[7] I, 4 (18).   [8] I, 5 (18).

twelve companions (as the conventional symbol of a fresh apostolate) he journeyed to Gaul seeking to find 'si salus ibi serenda sit', and if the Franks proved obdurate, 'ad vicinas nationes pertransire'.[1] Observing little 'poenitentiae medicamenta' in the country, he became an evangelist so that 'verbum evangelicum adnuntiaret'.[2] But with his community he continued the monastic life, 'ita ut in humanam conversationem angelicam agi vitam cerneres',[3] and he made his settlement in a wilderness far from human kind—'heremum petit'.[4] When banished from Luxeuil to Besançon, he found some condemned criminals in prison, preached to them, struck off their fetters, and led them to the local church, where the astonished guards discovered the entire party engaged in penitential exercises;[5] this was doubtless an act of evangelism, but the converted criminals were expected to behave, at least temporarily, like monks. When exiled to Bregenz, Columban agreed to settle there 'ob fidem in gentibus serendam';[6] and he later thought of preaching to the Veneti and Sclavi, but was divinely guided into Italy,[7] where he ended his life in theological confrontation with the Arians.[8]

Roussel[9] has pointed out that Columban was inspired by two motives—to push renunciation to extreme limits, both in leaving his own country, and in taking the Gospel to pagans and apostates. Thus pilgrimage and mission were united in the practice of monastic renunciation, and as Roussel continues, it is wrong to follow some German historians in questioning his missionary work. But this was a by-product of his primary purpose, resulting from the fact that Gaul even then was 'pays de mission'; and the worship of God remained the chief occupation of his monks, whose monasteries were deliberately founded in remote and uncultivated regions.

The concept of pilgrimage has had an ancient and prolonged history. St Augustine also uses the word *viator*, especially in his

---

[1] I, 5 (20).   [2] I, 6 (22).
[3] I, 6 (24).   [4] I, 7 (24).
[5] I, 23 (64).   [6] I, 31 (94).
[7] I, 32 (98).   [8] I, 35 (104).
[9] J. Roussel, *Saint Colomban* (1941), I, 99 n. 6.

sermons,[1] and compares the 'peregrinatio' of human life to the 'transitus per eremum' of the chosen people.[2] Indeed, the terrestrial part of the *Civitas Dei* is constantly on pilgrimage towards the land of true peace, joy, and eternity.[3] Bede[4] mentions a certain Egbert who 'in Hibernia diutius exulaverat pro Christo', remaining there until the end of his life as 'peregrinus pro Domino', with the main objective of reaching heaven—'pro adipiscenda in caelis patria'—but also with the subordinate desire to help others 'gentibus evangelizando'. Here again, pilgrimage and mission were ideally combined, although Egbert was in fact prevented by a divine vision from going as a missionary to the Continent. But Oursel[5] completely misunderstands or ignores the Irish of the early Middle Ages, when he defines pilgrimage as 'l'acte volontaire et désintéressé par lequel un homme abandonne ses lieux coutumiers...pour se rendre, dans un esprit religieux, jusqu'au sanctuaire qu'il s'est délibérément choisi ou qui lui a été imposé'. The Irish pilgrims—and Columban may be taken as representative of most—looked for no sanctuary on earth. They sought a heavenly country, and pilgrimage is described in their *Vitae*[6] as being 'pro Dei amore, propter nomen Domini, ob amorem Christi, pro remedio animae, pro adipiscenda in caelis patria, pro aeterna patria'. This Irish love of roaming was a Christianized version of the immemorial Celtic *Wanderlust*, expressed in English by Kenneth Macleod:[7]

> All the wonders 'yont our croft-dykes
> I will see, if I but may.
> All the ships that sail to Lochlann
> I will steer, if I but may.
> All the sunsets 'yont the Coolins
> I will reach, if I but may.

But the urge to travel was turned into Christian channels, so that pilgrimage became associated with mission, and both were subordinate to the spiritual perfection of the monk.

[1] G. B. Ladner, 'Alienation and Order', in *Speculum*, XLII (1967), 236 n. 14.
[2] Sermo 363; see B. de Gaiffier, in *Convegni*, IV (1963), 17 n. 8.
[3] *De civ. Dei*, I, *praefatio; Enchiridion*, 56 (15). [4] *HE*, III, 4; IV, 3; V, 9.
[5] R. Oursel, *Les Pélerins du Moyen Age* (1963), p. 9.
[6] Cf. *S. Columbani Opera*, p. xviii. [7] *The Road to the Isles* (1927), p. 49.

In some respects Columban foreshadows a crusader like St Louis, who died at Tunis singing 'Nous irons en Jerusalem'. His thought is parallel to the O *quanta qualia*[1] of Peter Abelard:

Nostrum est interim mentem erigere
Et totis patriam votis appetere,
Et ad Jerusalem a Babylonia
Post longa regredi tandem exilia.

Indeed, his poem *De Mundi Transitu* is strangely prophetic of that great hymn by an anonymous author of the thirteenth century[2] (which Puck[3] sang to the children as they left the enchanted forest, his voice tolling like a deep bell through the twilight):

Cur mundus militat sub vana gloria
Cuius prosperitas est transitoria?
Tam cito labitur eius potentia
Quam vasa figuli quae sunt fragilia.

Celtic pilgrimage was very different from the ideal of Benedictine monasticism. By his emphasis on stability and on diocesan supervision, St Benedict gave to his houses a static and local character. Columban, on the other hand, took the world as his parish, and followed the Irish practice in exempting his monks from episcopal control. At one period of European history, his Rule bade fair to rival that of Benedict; if it had prevailed, the history of monasticism (and with it, that of the medieval Church at large) might have been significantly different.

And so I reaffirm my verdict on Columban, which Ezio Franceschini[4] has translated into his own Italian: 'un monaco per vocazione, reso apostolo dalle circostanze'.

[1] In F. J. E. Raby, *Christian-Latin Poetry* (1927), p. 323.
[2] Raby, p. 435.
[3] R. Kipling, *Puck of Pook's Hill* (1939 ed.), p. 162.
[4] In the preface to Tosi's edition of Jonas, p. xi.

ST BONIFACE AND THE GERMAN MISSION

by C. H. TALBOT

O N this, the anniversary of the bringing to Mainz of the martyred body of St Boniface, it seems appropriate that any remarks about the Anglo-Saxon mission to Germany should be confined to his activities alone. Unfortunately, the story of his life has been told by many people at many times, and in default of new facts and documents, it is not possible to do more than repeat what is already well known.

To me the life of St Boniface appears to fall into three main periods: his mission from Gregory II to preach the gospel 'ad quascumque gentes infidelitatis errore detentas'; his work in Thuringia among a partly christianized people; and his organization of the Church in Germany together with the reform of the Frankish Church. In other words, his activities as priest, as bishop, and as archbishop. These three divisions illustrate not only the problems he had to face, but also the methods with which he attacked them.

The fundamental prerequisite of a missionary, one might think, is that he be sent: *missus*. Yet Boniface, or Wynfryth as he was originally called, was not sent by anyone when he undertook his first journey into Frisia. It was a purely personal enterprise. Certainly he set out with permission from his abbot and community. But his journey overseas was by no means an official expedition, sponsored by authority and assured of external support. On the other hand it was not an enterprise precipitated by sudden impulse or emotional enthusiasm. Though his action may have contained some element of the Celtic 'peregrinatio pro Christo', it was not instigated by a penitential urge or a desire for personal perfection. It was conceived solely as an attempt to spread the Gospel, to bring pagans within the bosom of the

Church. To carry out this purpose he had prepared himself carefully under the discipline of monastic life, first as disciple, then as teacher, and finally as a member of ecclesiastical synods. Consequently, he was well equipped for his task, a mature, learned, and adequately experienced man.

His first journey, embarked upon with two or three companions, ended after only one year with very little accomplished. Though he had been well received by his pagan hosts, he had not been allowed to push his work forward. To some his venture may have seemed a complete failure. But to Boniface it was an exploratory probe that was to prove invaluable for his future work. From it he learned several important truths: first, that without the official backing of an authority which would vouch for the genuineness of his mission, there were problems which simple enthusiasm and good will could not resolve. For the continental kings, dukes, bishops, and abbots had seen far too many Celtic visitors wandering about from place to place, whipping up the interest of their subjects, baptizing them, and then, on a sudden whim, leaving them to their own devices, bereft of help or guidance. They had seen far too many adventurers passing themselves off as bishops and priests from distant lands, only to discover later that they were impostors. Credentials regarding ordination, source of authority, purpose, and a de-limited field of activity were an absolute necessity if missionary work was to be successful. Secondly, he realized that a permanent mission must have proper organization to secure any degree of stability. Friendly and hospitable people might provide the missioner from time to time with food and shelter; but in alien and oftentimes antagonistic areas complete material independence was imperative. To be self-contained, therefore, the missioners must have assistants devoting themselves entirely to the corporal needs of the preachers, and they must have close ties with their homeland, from which they could receive support.

Thirdly, political factors might sometimes prove more difficult to surmount than doctrinal ones; indeed, they might render missionary work completely impossible. In regions, for instance, which had been conquered by the Franks, Christianity and alien rule were synonymous. Whereas paganism was equated with freedom and independence, Christianity was linked with subservience and oppression. The missionary, therefore, though personally disinterested in political movements, must conciliate and ally himself with whatever political power could further his aims.

When Boniface embarked on his second missionary journey, his plans were better laid. On this occasion he armed himself with letters of recommendation from his diocesan bishop, Daniel of Winchester and, as if that were not enough, he betook himself to Rome to solicit from the Pope even more awesome authority for his enterprise. Gregory II made a rigorous enquiry into his motives, his competence, and his background, but eventually granted him a commission expressed in the widest terms of reference, namely to preach 'to whatever people he encountered entangled in the errors of heathendom'. The only conditions attached to this commission were, that he teach the Old and New Testament, that he confine himself to the established doctrines of the Church (especially regarding baptism), and that he conform to the fixed ecclesiastical customs. Furthermore, his mission was to be carried out in a spirit of virtue, love, and sobriety. All this was to be done *ratione consona*, in accordance with reason.

Boniface immediately departed for Thuringia. But hardly had his work begun than he heard of the death of Radbod, the political obstacle to his earlier mission in Frisia. Abandoning his own plans, he put himself at the disposal of Willibrord, his precursor in this field, and for three years toiled faithfully and with success. He might never have forsaken this work, had not Willibrord, now ageing and desperately in need of a suitable successor for his see, brought pressure to bear on Boniface to accept episcopal consecration. Boniface extricated himself from this difficult position by referring to canon law, which demanded that episcopal candidates be fifty years of age, and he reinforced his excuse by alleging the obedience owed to Gregory II for his original commission. With that, he returned to Germany.

The moment had now come when he would have to work

on his own responsibility. Before him stretched an almost limit-
less field of labour, the vast country east of the Rhine. Some of it
was ruled by Frankish vassals and was still half pagan; some of
it, like Saxony, was completely so. He turned his attention first
to Hesse and Thuringia, a land of impenetrable forests and ancient
barbarism. Missionaries, mostly Irish (of whom St Kilian was
still held in veneration), had already worked there. But the
indifference of the Merovingian kings, the lack of organization,
possibly too the extreme austerity of the Irish with their peculiar
ideas on liturgy and discipline, had impeded the full growth and
flowering of Christianity. A completely perverted form of religion
had taken root. The worship of idols under a Christian guise, the
sacrificial rites to Thor performed by ostensibly Christian priests,
with all their accompanying superstitions, auguries, incantations,
wearing of amulets, and the like, presented Boniface with problems which he had never encountered before.

In his earlier missionary work in Frisia he had been confronted
with people whose religion was polytheistic. Not only had they
a whole hierarchy of gods, but between them and the everyday
world there flourished a host of elves, spirits, departed souls,
witches, and demons, all of whom were thought to influence
and determine the course of human affairs. Though these people
lived in a spirit world, it was far from being a spiritual one.
It was deeply materialistic, concerned solely with affairs of earthly
prosperity and bodily satisfaction. It presented a complete contrast to the Christian ideals of personal self-sacrifice, of suffering
for God's sake, of performing good works for a supernatural
reward. So between missioner and pagan there was not merely
a doctrinal difference, but a deeper psychological gulf as well.

At first Boniface was inclined to deal with this state of affairs
in a simple, direct and, one might say, violent manner. He
destroyed the temples and shrines, smashed the sacred stones in
pieces, and hewed down the trees that the pagans held in veneration. Rough and crude as this approach might appear, it had
a logic of its own. For if the physical and sensible objects, to
which the pagans attributed so much power, could be destroyed
without any apparent retribution from the gods, then the

impotence of the pagan deities was made clearly manifest. Conversely, the power of the Christian god was convincingly proved. In Frisia and Hesse Boniface had pursued these tactics, basing his actions on the example of Willibrord and earlier missionaries. But gradually he began to lose faith in this aggressive approach, and after communicating his doubts to Bishop Daniel of Winchester, he received the advice which he later adopted.

It was a mistake, Daniel wrote, to provoke the pagans and to remove from them, with force, the objects to which they were attached. It was better to ask them questions about their gods, to enquire about their origins, their seemingly human attributes, their relationship with the beginning of the world, and in so doing elicit such contradictions and absurdities from their answers that they would become confused and ashamed. Rational argument would convince the pagans of their errors more successfully than the destruction of their sacred shrines, and its effects would be more lasting. This advice, inspired by that given to St Augustine on his first mission to England, was accepted; but it seems strange, considering Boniface's undoubted learning, that he had not recalled it earlier.

Of his dealings with the more intractable problem of revitalizing Christian ideas perverted by paganism we have no evidence. He succeeded, however, with the assistance of two sympathetic, half-Christian, half-pagan rulers in converting many thousands from their inveterate heathen practices, and sent a report of his success to Rome. There can be no doubt that this report, no longer extant, contained many questions concerning the day-to-day problems of his ministry, and particularly those connected with perverted forms of Christian practice. The immediate outcome of this report was a summons to Rome, a searching interrogation on his beliefs, his teaching, and the customs of the people he was evangelizing, and his final consecration as bishop.

This was not a case of becoming a bishop like anyone else. Boniface had no diocese, no episcopal see, no attachment or subordination to a metropolitan. His sphere of work was the whole of Germany beyond the Rhine: his flock comprised everyone, pagans as well as Christians, who lived in that area.

He was given a kind of roving commission under the direct supervision of the Holy See, to which he was solely responsible. But his additional powers as bishop meant that he could confirm those neophytes whom he had baptized into the Christian faith, could ordain suitable candidates to the priesthood and so enlarge the scope of his work, and could apply canon law to any priests within his jurisdiction. It is not without significance that, at his consecration, he was given a copy of Dionysius Exiguus, a collection of Church councils, which would facilitate this task. At the same time he was furnished with a letter of recommendation to Charles Martel, from whom, shortly afterwards, he received full protection. This protection was not absolutely necessary for the conversion of the pagans, but it was invaluable for securing Boniface from that open opposition, shown by certain lords and rulers, which had hitherto thwarted his most strenuous efforts. Later he was to acknowledge that 'without the protection of the Prince of the Franks I should not have been able to rule the people of the church, to defend the priests, monks, and nuns, nor to forbid sacrilegious rites and the worship of idols'.

On his return from Rome, Boniface began to think of his ministry in wider terms. He had already built a small monastery at Amöneburg dedicated to St Michael, and he now constructed another at Ohrdruf. This was part of a plan to establish centres for training aspirants to the monastic life. He recalled that Willibrord had adopted this plan in Frisia, when he brought back from Denmark thirty young men to be educated as future members of his missionary band: and he himself, during his sojourn at the monastery of Pfalzel, had recruited a Frankish youth named Gregory, who was later to become Abbot of Utrecht. He now decided to pursue this recruitment of younger men on a larger scale. He was conscious that the mere conversion of people and the provision of churches for them to worship in was insufficient. What was needed in order to establish Christianity on a permanent footing was a succession of teachers of high calibre, imbued with a strong spirit of discipline, obedient to authority, and motivated by the highest spiritual ideals. Only within the framework of monastic life could these aims be attained. Moreover, the monasteries would provide perfect examples of the Christian life to people living in the neighbourhood, so that what they could not learn through words they could imbibe through example. To ensure the success of this plan Boniface forged even closer links with monasteries in England. Since the outset of his mission on the Continent he had kept up a correspondence with abbots, nuns, and monks, many of whom provided him with books. Now, in his capacity as bishop, he made greater claims on their sympathy and assistance, and he attracted to his side enthusiastic helpers of every kind. Priests, monks, nuns, teachers, men skilled in various arts, 'in exceedingly large numbers', as Willibald tells us, came to join in his work and put themselves under his jurisdiction.

So for a time his mission was assured. He built the abbey of Fritzlar, to which were soon added three convents for nuns: Bischofsheim under Leoba, Kitzingen and Ochsenfurt under Thecla. These were to form the operational bases from which the moral and cultural education of the Germans was to be achieved.

It was at this period, four years after his consecration, that Boniface received a letter from Gregory II answering a number of questions which Boniface had proposed to him. This letter, like most of those in Boniface's correspondence, may appear at first sight to be pernickety, to be concerned with insignificant details. There are no matters concerning faith and doctrine, except perhaps those on baptism. But this should not surprise us, for in the primitive conditions in which he was working, deep theological controversies about the Trinity, about the hypostatic union, the sacrament of the altar, and such mysteries were not likely to arise. Most of Boniface's queries hinged on Church discipline: questions about degrees of affinity, about the segregation of lepers, about eating meat sacrificed to idols, about the separation of husband and wife in cases of sickness, and so on. Such details may appear to be of little import compared with other problems. But to the mind of Boniface they were crucial. When he had taken the oath of office at his consecration, he had sworn on the Gospels not to depart in any way from the unity of the universal Church. This, to him, meant not merely the fundamental dogmas of the Church which are formulated in the Creed, but also the decrees passed by popes and councils long ago. As keeper of the law of the Church he felt bound to observe these decrees down to their smallest detail. Furthermore, for whatever decision he took on these points of detail he desired to have the support of the highest authority he knew. His Irish and Frankish predecessors had pleased themselves, to some extent, how they interpreted both doctrine and discipline. They had acted independently of authority, arrogating to themselves powers they did not possess, and leading astray those whom they were supposed to guide. Boniface's idea seemed to be that once the Christian faith had been adopted, one could not pick and choose those particular sections of it which suited oneself, but that the whole corpus of doctrine, authority, tradition, and discipline must be accepted without question.

Nor was it merely a question of observing the niceties of ecclesiastical law. There was the ever-important question of keeping the peace, *servantes unitatem in vinculo pacis*. Many quarrels had arisen through disagreement on small points of Church law. It did not escape Boniface that such apparently simple questions as the computation of Easter or the wearing of a special form of tonsure could drive a deep wedge between two bodies of sincere believers, both pursuing with equal zest the Christian ideal. Consequently, in conditions where Christians were still on a shaky footing, it was imperative that no rifts should occur, which might lead pagans to believe that Christians could not agree on their own doctrines and behaviour. Signs of disagreement could only lead to lack of confidence, indifference, and scepticism, especially among the weaker members of a newly converted society. So the authority of Rome, the sanctity of the Holy See, was the ultimate appeal of Boniface on all doubtful points of law. We even find him writing at one juncture to four different people to discover the true interpretation of a canon. He was unaware, he said, that spiritual relationship, as between a godfather and the mother of his godson, was a diriment impediment to marriage. He had searched the ancient canons, the decrees of the popes, and the *calculus peccatorum* without discovering any foundation for the belief, held by his Frankish colleagues, that marriage between two such persons was an incestuous relationship. Pehtelm of Whithorn, Nothelm of Canterbury, Abbot Duddo, and the Pope were all asked what he should do in this matter. It was fortunate that Boniface acted so prudently. For later he discovered that such a marriage was considered a heinous offence in the Frankish kingdom, punishable by death. Had he allowed such a marriage to take place, he could have been convicted not only of transgressing the ecclesiastical law, but of flouting also the laws of his political master. This might have led to the withdrawal of protection, the weakening of Boniface's position as leader of the Church in Germany, and the breakdown of his missionary work.

A new phase in the career of Boniface was marked by the accession of Gregory III to the papal throne. Having written, as was his custom, to congratulate the Pope on his appointment, Boniface was sent the pallium and thereby became archbishop. This considerably enlarged the scope of his missionary work. Germany would no longer be a mere diocese directed and ruled by one man: it would become a province divided into several dioceses and governed by a number of bishops.

Boniface addressed himself to this task in 732, but it was not until his return from a visit to Rome in 738 that he was able to bring it to a satisfactory conclusion. In that year he travelled to Rome with a great retinue, stayed there for a whole year, and attended a solemn Church council. When he reached Germany once more in 739 he began to organize the bishoprics in Bavaria, a fairly easy operation, since the country had been Christian for several generations, thanks to the preaching of St Rupert and St Corbinian, and only twenty years previously had been visited by papal legates. Here he established three bishoprics, Salzburg, Freising, and Ratisbon. In Hesse and Thuringia the task was more difficult, not only because of the relatively recent conversion of the people, but also because of the lack of large towns. Nevertheless, near the monasteries of Fritzlar and Amöneburg in Hesse he established the bishopric of Buraburg, and in Thuringia he made two dioceses, one in the north at Erfurt near the abbey of

Ohrdruf, the other in the south at Wurzburg. Only the northern part of Bavaria remained without a see, so at Eichstatt he installed Willibald, the hero of the *Hodoeporicon*, soon to be joined by his brother Wynnebald and his sister Walburga, who ruled over the convent at Heidenheim. In this way the whole of the German Church was organized and incorporated into the universal Church.

By the year 742, when all this had been accomplished and when it seemed that Boniface might enjoy some rest from his labours, he came face to face with an enormous problem, the reformation and reorganization of the Frankish Church. Few pages of history can show a darker picture than that presented by the Church and clergy in the Frankish kingdom at that time. Boniface's correspondence is one long cry of anguish and indignation at the scandals and abuses of which he was often a helpless witness. His troubles in Hesse and Thuringia had been bitter, but they were as nothing compared with what he found in the Frankish Church.

Church life was almost at a standstill. The councils which in the sixth century had constituted a great civilizing influence (Agde in 506, Orleans in 511, Epaone in 517) had fallen into disuse; some episcopal sees were abandoned, others were in the hands of unprincipled clerics or layfolk; bishops openly admitted to having several concubines, were drunken, spent their days in hunting, or carried arms in battle, killing with true ecclesiastical impartiality both pagans and Christians. The lower clergy was no better: their ignorance, venality and immorality were manifest. Slaves escaping from their masters had themselves tonsured and served churches; adventurers wandered about seducing the people with heterodox teachings; and what added to the confusion was the troop of Irish or Breton priests from overseas who drifted from diocese to diocese, subject to no ecclesiastical authority, living as they pleased and insisting on their national customs.

Boniface, confronted with this state of affairs, seems to have had no hesitation in choosing his weapon of attack. It was the Church council. Though he wrote to Pope Zacharias that he had been invited by Carloman to hold a council in his kingdom, we may be certain (and indeed his biographer insists upon it) that Boniface was the prime mover. What he was asking from the Pope in this instance was a directive and instruction, so that both should agree on one and the same point.

Here begins what can be called the conciliar movement in the Frankish Empire. Under Carloman two councils were held, one in 742 at an unidentified place, another at Estinnes in Hainault in 743. In the following year Pepin the Short, imitating his brother's attempts at reform, called a council at Soisson, which reproduced in great measure the ordinances of the two Austrasian synods. Then to crown the work, a general council of all the Frankish Empire was held in 745. These four councils brought order out of chaos, suppressed abuses, enforced discipline, and gave back to the Church a sense of respect and dignity. Over all these councils Boniface presided in his capacity as legate of the Holy See. In effect it was his life's programme that was being carried out—freeing the layfolk from ignorance and superstition, bringing the clergy to acknowledge their responsibilities, organizing the bishops, and coordinating their efforts with those of the Holy See. But in this instance he was working from the top downwards, not, as he had done in heathenish lands, from the bottom upwards. Within five years he had transformed a scene of disaster into one of order and beauty, and the permanence of this transformation was assured by one final council of the whole Empire in 747, when all the reforms of the earlier councils were confirmed and enforced.

At this moment of triumph Boniface was not unmindful of the benefits which could accrue to the land of his birth, should such reforms be followed there. He therefore wrote to Cuthbert, Archbishop of Canterbury, communicating the resolutions passed by the Frankish bishops and encouraging him to take the same steps. It was probably on his advice that Pope Zacharias wrote twice to Cuthbert in the same vein, and through him that the Council of Cloveshoe took place.

In the midst of these labours he was preoccupied with the foundation of the abbey of Fulda, which received its charter of donation 12 January 744. Earlier he had sent Sturm, one of his young oblates, to Rome, Monte Cassino, and other abbeys in

Tuscany to learn all he could about the practice of the Benedictine Rule, and now he placed him in charge of Fulda. Situated as the monastery was in the middle of the four peoples converted by Boniface—the Franks, Hessians, Thuringians, and Bavarians—it not only became the centre for continuing his work of evangelization in Germany, but stood as a symbol, embodying the idea that monastic life, with its discipline and self-sacrifice, lay at the heart of his missionary labours.

To sum up: as a priest Boniface had spent his energies in detaching pagans from their erroneous ideas and customs, and in instilling into them the rudiments of the Christian faith. As bishop his main concern was with the establishment of priestly standards, with the training of candidates to continue his work, with the observance of canon law, and with the ensuring of protection for his neophytes and helpers. As archbishop his aim was rather different. Now he was concerned not so much with the laity as with the bishops themselves, with the organization of countries into dioceses, the choice of suitable candidates for episcopal office, and with the convoking of councils where the bishops could impose discipline. Furthermore he was concerned with the reform of the whole Frankish Church, which for long had suffered from every kind of abuse. By convoking councils at which legislation could be enforced under the authority of the Emperor, by eliminating undesirable elements from places of ecclesiastical power, Boniface was to lay the foundations of medieval Europe. In his latter days his anxiety about the bishops comes constantly to the fore: 'I suffer most of all', he said, 'from false bishops, adulterous priests, and from immoral clerics of all grades', for though his ideas were praised by both Pope and Emperor, he was subjected to persecution from those who were most affected by his organizing and legislating activity. Later he was to say that he felt like a barking dog that sees his master's house broken into by robbers and systematically rifled: all he could do was to whine and show grief.

These complaints, if they can be so called, were justified by the treatment he received at the hands of members of the episcopate. After more than twenty-five years as bishop and thirteen as archbishop, he still possessed no stable see. Though he had laboriously revived the power of the metropolitan in the Frankish kingdom, there was still no metropolitan see in Germany. And when, on the death of Raginfried of Cologne, the time appeared propitious for him to take up this position, the crowning achievement of his work, the opposition from the immoral and simoniacal clergy was so strong that he was forced to renounce this hope.

Two further blows were to cause him deep grief: the metropolitan sees of Sens and Rheims disappeared in face of the same kind of opposition, and his vast diocese was devastated by the Saxons under the leadership of Carloman's brother, Gripho. Every step so painfully taken forward now seemed to have been taken in vain. With the connivance of his enemies, all the abuses which he had laboured to stamp out came to life once more, and he was even delated to Rome by envious bishops for rebaptizing children who had been christened 'in nomine patria et filia et spiritus sancti'. His declining years seemed fated to end in utter failure, with the destruction of all that he had fought for.

But a glorious end awaited him. Setting out with fifty-three companions for the land which had attracted him in early manhood, fired with the hope of converting the last remnants of the Frisian pagans to the Christian faith, he met his death, shielding himself from the attacker's sword with a copy of the Gospels.

THE MISSIONARY AT HOME:
THE CHURCH IN THE
TOWNS, 1000–1250

by C. N. L. BROOKE

THE wide span of years which I have boldly claimed in
my title is intended to enmesh and hold together for our
inspection the first great age of the medieval city, the
tenth and eleventh centuries, when the medieval Church first
faced the problem of evangelism in growing mercantile communities, and the age when it deployed in the cities and towns
of Europe a new army of missionaries in the persons of the
friars. The missionary techniques of the friars are familiar and
comparatively well documented; the evangelism of the tenth
and eleventh centuries is scarcely documented at all. In recent
years the dramatic nature of urban history in this early period
has been becoming increasingly apparent; and it was in the
conviction that the Church's hand in it could not wholly escape
detection that I chose the title for this lecture. Many aspects of
this problem have been traced with the closest care; but I justify
the breadth and cloudiness of my theme by a conviction that it
has rarely been looked at quite from this point of view.

Broadly speaking, St Dominic believed in evangelism by
preaching, St Francis in evangelism by example. To both, in the
long run, the whole world was their parish, though both concentrated on the towns of Western Christendom as their main
field of activity. The similarities and the contrasts are exceedingly
instructive; all the more so, I believe, for being deliberate. In the
ancient controversy as to whether Dominic was influenced by
Francis, I hold the heretical opinion that the influence was
powerful and decisive; but I am sure that Dominic took pains
to avoid the Franciscan model in some respects while following

it in others.[1] Late in 1216, if my reconstruction is correct, Dominic and Francis met in Rome; and Dominic was so impressed that he suggested that the two Orders be merged. Francis was by nature the more original and subtle, and he clearly appreciated that Dominic was a man of powerful mind in some ways quite different from his; in any event, he refused to absorb the Dominicans. At this stage Dominic's Order was a tiny community of Canons Regular, with a special instruction to preach. On his return to Toulouse, Dominic staged a revolution in his community: suddenly and without warning he dispersed them to the four winds. They turned their backs on the heretics among whom they had been working hitherto, and went out to preach to the Church at large; they became, as we understand the term, friars. Thus far, and in certain striking details, Dominic seems to be following Francis; but in looking to Paris and Bologna, the great student centres, for recruits and in devising over the years the most precise and sophisticated organization of its day, he was doing precisely the opposite of Francis. Dominic conceived an Order of instructed clerks—not an Order of high scholastics, but of trained men—who could travel and preach; and who, while not actually on the road or in the pulpit, would live an ordered, ascetic life on the Premonstratensian pattern in their convents. Francis's recruits were a cross-section of Italian society; but in early days the majority were simple laymen, townsfolk and peasants, who were commonly illiterate.

We clerks recited the office like other clerks [declared St Francis in his *Testament*]. The laymen recited the Pater Noster; and we dwelt in churches gladly, and were simple folk and subject to all men. And I worked, and wish to work, with my hands; and I firmly will that all other brothers work at a craft which is decent and good. Those

---

[1] See Brooke, *Trans. Roy. Hist. Soc.* 5th ser. XVII (1967)—henceforth Brooke (1967)—pp. 30 ff., especially p. 36. In all that relates to the friars I owe a special debt to my wife, Dr Rosalind Brooke, and to Professor Dom David Knowles, though neither is to be held responsible for the statement of my views; and for town parishes, among many who have helped me, I should like particularly to acknowledge my debt to Mrs G. Keir, Miss Susan Reynolds, Professor D. A. Bullough (see p. 64 n. 4) and Professor R. B. Pugh. For what follows, see ibid. and C. N. L. Brooke in *Bull. Inst. Hist. Res.* XLI (1968), 115–31, especially p. 130 —henceforth Brooke (1968).

who know none, let them learn, not out of greed for labour's reward, but *as an example* and to drive out idleness. And when we are not given the reward of our toil, let us turn back to God's table and seek alms from door to door.[1]

Francis himself preached, to humans as well as to animals; but he never regarded preaching as his own main function or that of his Order. Still less was he an organizer; he was there to give an example. Preachers formed a small minority in early days, and it was something of a puzzle to those not in the Franciscan secret, so to speak, what the function of most friars was. Dominic refused to recruit illiterate laymen; the hierarchy viewed groups of such folk with suspicion, as men inadequately prepared to resist heresy. The leaders of the northern provinces who started the revolt against Brother Elias in the 1230s, the men who admired learning and committee government and all things Dominican, were equally baffled; and their central figure, Hamo of Faversham, inspired a decree in General Chapter forbidding the recruitment of laymen in this sense.[2] By the time that Salimbene came to write his chronicle, they were virtually an extinct species even in Italy, and he describes those he had met in early days with raised eyebrows and without regret. 'They were useless for hearing confessions...They did nothing but eat and sleep.'[3]

Francis, on the other hand, repeatedly emphasized that lay brothers, by their prayers and their example, formed the centre of his Order. It is clear that he was determined to heal the rift between clergy and laity; that he took seriously the danger inherent in the separation of layman and cleric which had been so conspicuous a feature of the papal reform of the eleventh century and its aftermath. The well-educated clergy moved into a high social stratum in a hierarchical society, and if they preached to the poor their words tended to pass over their audience's heads; the rank and file of the clergy failed to live up to the modes and ideals of the papal reform, and were by that token despised and rejected and demoralized. The function of the Franciscans was

[1] *Opuscula S. Patris Francisci Assisiensis* (2nd ed. Quaracchi, 1941), p. 79.
[2] See R. B. Brooke, *Early Franciscan Government*, pp. 243 ff.
[3] Ed. O. Holder-Egger, *MGH, Scriptores*, xxxii, 1905–13, p. 102.

to fill this gap; like worker priests to live among ordinary folk on their own terms. In a world in which under-employment, poverty, and starvation were always at the door, and which lacked the material resources or techniques for curing any of them, it was worse than useless to preach acceptance and submission: Francis's vision and originality consisted in sending out men who rejoiced in poverty as a positive, exciting, romantic thing; who were happy to be poorer than the poor, humbler than the humble, more ignorant than the ignorant. In high society, the romantic subjection to female tyranny portrayed in many romances was the reverse, the deliberate ironic parody of the high society of fact, in which women were commonly drudges and slaves, slaves of the marriage market, of the marriage bed, and of the ludicrous dynastic ambitions of their menfolk. But they gained some relief from the literary cult which portrayed them in a contrary role. To abolish poverty was beyond the range of possible imagination in the thirteenth century; but some reconciliation between the doctrine that the world was God's world and the horror of everyday experience could be effected by making poverty a holy thing.[1]

This presupposed a missionary strategy which is essentially silent and subtle; which works by example more than by preaching. There is a striking similarity in this respect between Francis's general missionary strategy and his particular treatment of heresy. It has commonly been supposed that Dominic was interested in heretics, and especially in the Cathars, and Francis not; for Dominic devoted his best energies to preaching against them, and they hardly figure in Francis's writings or the early lives. But if we ask the simple question, which is likely to have known more of the Cathars, the native of old Castile or the merchant's son of Assisi, we must surely say Francis. The valley of Spoleto boasted, or hid, a Cathar bishop; two or three years before Francis's conversion Assisi apparently had a Cathar *podestà*; Pietro Bernardone traded over the ground where they grew

---

[1] Cf. the studies of M. Mollat, especially 'La notion de la pauvreté au moyen âge: position de problèmes', *Revue d'histoire de l'Église de France*, CXLIX (1966), 1–17, and references there stated.

thickest.[1] Francis taught, and above all lived, the Catholic life, saying nothing of the heretics, but quietly turning his back on them; Dominic engaged, in early years, in public disputation with them. I suppose we would normally reckon today that Francis had understood the problem better than Dominic; I am sure that Dominic himself supposed so.

If we seek to trace out their attitude, we can study Francis's writings, Dominic's constitutions, the lives of both men, and the comments of their contemporaries.[2] Almost all the evidence by which we may compare the attitude of the men who worked in the rising towns two or three centuries before is indirect. Much of my paper must therefore consist of an attempt to sketch the framework of churches and parishes in the towns; only with such a basis can one hope to penetrate into a very obscure world of religious activity.

It may be wondered whether there is a subject here at all; whether we can hope to know enough about the work of the Church in eleventh-century towns to justify the enterprise. We have, at least, some puzzles on our hands, and they may make a promising beginning. Let me sketch two contrasts. When the men who had the invidious task of assessing the English Church for papal taxation in 1254 came to the diocese of Ely, they found in Cambridge fifteen parish churches, in Ely one; yet they decided, rightly or wrongly, that the one parish in Ely was worth more than the fifteen in Cambridge put together.[3] This does not mean that Ely was a larger or more prosperous place than Cambridge; no doubt the reverse was true. A mercantile community might

---

[1] Cf. Brooke (1968)—above, p. 60 n. 1; K. Esser in *Archivum Franciscanum Historicum*, LI (1958), especially p. 239; A. Borst, *Die Katharer* (Stuttgart 1953), pp. 231 ff.

[2] On the Dominican sources, see Brooke (1967); on the Constitutions, ibid. p. 28 n. and references cited, especially P. Mandonnet and M.-H. Vicaire, *Saint Dominique, l'idée, l'homme et l'oeuvre* (Paris 1937), II, 203 ff., 273 ff.; G. R. Galbraith, *The Constitution of the Dominican Order, 1216–1360* (Manchester 1925).

[3] *Valuation of Norwich*, ed. W. E. Lunt (Oxford 1926), pp. 212, 218–19. On the early history of parishes in general G. W. O. Addleshaw, *Beginnings of the Parochial System*, St Anthony's Hall Publications, no. 9 (York 1956), and the excellent bibliography of D. Kurze, *Pfarrerwahlen im Mittelalter: Ein Beitrag zur Geschichte der Gemeinde und des Niederkirchenwesens* (Cologne–Graz 1966).

have large wealth by the thirteenth century but little tithe.[1] Nonetheless, it points a striking contrast. No doubt we shall rehearse numerous explanations—social, economic and legal— before we claim that the men of Cambridge were of more conspicuous piety than those of Ely; but a church at every street corner is a puzzle in any age.

In 1092 the most ancient persons of the three counties adjacent to Worcester sat for three days in the crypt of Worcester Cathedral, and decided in the end that Worcester city contained only one parish, that of the mother church, the cathedral, even though it had other and ancient churches.[2] No doubt this was an antique decision, and represented the most conservative point of view as to the number of parishes in the city, combined with a forward-looking view of the rights of the Church, of the status in canon law of bishop and parish priest. To this we shall return; for the moment, let us observe the contrast.

In many parts of Europe a jury of ancients would have given a very similar answer in the late eleventh century. In Italy, for example, it was normal for even a large town to remain a single parish down to the twelfth century; and some small Italian cathedral cities have only one parish to this day.[3] In the larger cities churches might proliferate: in 924 the Magyars are said to have destroyed 44 churches in Pavia alone, and it is certain that there were something like this number in the city at that time.[4]

[1] In theory, tithes were paid on all kinds of income, and the extent to which non-agricultural tithe disappeared in the twelfth and thirteenth centuries may have been exaggerated; but it is certainly from the twelfth century that this tendency grew (see G. Constable, *Monastic tithes from their origins to the twelfth century* (Cambridge 1964), pp. 16 ff., especially 17 n. 1; 267–8, especially 268 n. 1; 287 ff.). Professor Constable's book is the indispensable recent guide to the tangled history of tithes, although it only covers part of the field: see ibid. p. 1 n. 1, for general books on the subject of this paper. C. Boyd, *Tithes and Parishes in Medieval Italy* (Ithaca 1952), is of particular interest.

[2] Ed. R. R. Darlington, *Cartulary of Worcester Cathedral Priory* (Pipe Roll Society, 1968), pp. 31–2; cf. idem, *The Vita Wulfstani of William of Malmesbury* (Camden Third Series, XL, 1928), pp. xxxvii, 191.

[3] See Boyd, p. 53 n. 12; cf. p. 84.

[4] See D. A. Bullough, 'Urban Change in early Medieval Italy: the example of Pavia', *Papers of the British School at Rome*, XXXIV (1966), esp. pp. 99, 119 ff. I am much indebted to Professor Bullough for discussing some of the problems

In Europe at large this would seem a sensational number for the early tenth century, even if small compared with the 133 described by Opicino in Pavia in the fourteenth century.[1] This illustrates the obvious fact that there may be far more churches than parishes, and that in Italy, unlike parts of northern Europe, there was no tendency in the central Middle Ages for parishes to split, so that eventually the churches which survived had each its parish. In Italy, indeed, it was no uncommon thing to have more than one cathedral in a city. The extreme case was, of course, Rome: the Lateran Basilica may be the Pope's cathedral as bishop of the city, but as Pope he has five; and one could say that, just as the altars of the major basilicas were like the major altars of a single cathedral, so the titular churches, the parish churches of the cardinal priests, operated like the side chapels or chantry chapels of a late medieval cathedral. Their incardination[2] in the papal basilicas made them all members of the chapter of the mother church; and in that sense the Roman scene was as elsewhere in Italy—a single cathedral community dominated all the city churches. But the cardinals were parish priests or arch-priests before they had been incardinated into the basilicas, and in that sense provided the pattern and exemplar for the parochial system in the later medieval pattern. The cathedral clergy of Rome were unique in being nomadic; but transhumance was not uncommon in Italy—in Pavia, for instance, there was a summer and a winter cathedral.[3]

A pilgrim to Rome from north-western Europe in the late

of this paper with me, and for valuable advice and references. His study of early Pavia provides an excellent illustration of what the evidence for a well-documented Italian city can reveal. An interesting parallel to Pavia is Dorstad, which is said to have had 55 churches before its destruction in the ninth century (see P. Johansen, 'Die Kaufmanskirche im Ostseegebiet' in *Studien zu den Anfängen des europäischen Städtewesens*, Vorträge und Forschungen, ed. T. Mayer (Lindau–Constance 1958), pp. 499–525 (cf. p. 78 n. 1).

[1] *Liber de Laudibus civitatis Ticinensis*, ed. R. Maiocchi and F. Quintavalle, *Rerum Italicarum Scriptores*, XI, i (1903), 4 ff., especially p. 17 (133, excluding chapels, 'intra urbem', c. 34 in the suburbs); also ed. F. Gianani (Pavia 1927), pp. 77 ff., 91.

[2] See S. Kuttner, 'Cardinalis: the History of a Canonical Concept', *Traditio*, III (1945), 129–214.

[3] Cf. Bullough (see p. 64 n.), p. 100.

eleventh century might well have been bewildered by the variety which he found. In the west of England occasionally cities like Worcester had already a group of churches; but normally one parish as yet, and commonly (as in Hereford) only one church before the twelfth century.[1] In the eastern part of England he would find churches very numerous and commonly already very independent: in Lincoln some thirty-five churches already by 1100, which was to rise to nearly fifty by the end of the twelfth century: in York fourteen at least by 1100, rising to nearly forty by 1200.[2] London had probably already the largest number of parish churches of any city in Christendom, and they were rising fast; by the late twelfth century it had well over a hundred parish churches strictly so called within the area of the city walls.[3] In parts of France he would find a situation comparable to Cambridge or Canterbury—with a moderate number of parishes rapidly increasing; thus Poitiers and Bourges (to take two cases which have been systematically investigated) each had twenty or thirty parish churches by the eleventh century.[4] But in the Low Countries, Burgundy, the Rhineland, and south-western Germany in general, he would rarely have found a multiplicity of town churches, let alone of parishes.[5] In Cologne some sort of parochial division of the area within the ancient walls may go

[1] On Hereford see Mrs M. D. Dobel in *Historic Towns*, 1, (London–Oxford 1969).

[2] On Lincoln see Sir J. W. F. Hill, *Medieval Lincoln* (Cambridge 1948), pp. 147 ff.; on York, *Victoria County History* (henceforth *VCH, York*), pp. 365 ff.

[3] See F. M. Stenton, *Norman London*, p. 40 and map (rev. ed. Historical Association, 1934, with map by Miss M. B. Honeybourne, and notes by Miss E. Jeffries Davis; repr. without the map, in *Social Life in Early England*, ed. G. Barraclough, London 1960, pp. 179 ff.); cf. Brooke, *Time the archsatirist* (London 1968), pp. 17 ff. Mrs G. Keir and I are preparing a detailed study of the early history of the London parishes.

[4] D. Claude, *Topographie und Verfassung der Städte Bourges und Poitiers bis in das 11. Jahrhundert*, Hist. Studien, 380 (Lübeck u. Hamburg 1960), *passim*, especially the maps facing p. 196. For Canterbury see W. Urry, *Canterbury under the Angevin Kings* (London 1967), pp. 207 ff., especially 210–11.

[5] F. L. Ganshof, *Étude sur le développement des villes entre Loire et Rhin au moyen âge* (Paris–Brussels 1943), pp. 47 ff.; W Müller, 'Pfarrei und mittelalterliche Stadt in Bereiche Südbadens', *Neue Beiträge zur südwestdeutschen Landesgeschichte: Festschrift für Max Miller* (Stuttgart 1962), pp. 69–80. Of exceptional interest is the history of Paris, on which see A. Friedmann, *Paris: ses rues, ses paroisses du moyen âge à la Révolution* (Paris 1959).

back to the ninth century: if so, it is the earliest documented division of a city into parishes in Western Christendom. Even in Cologne there was no approximation to the English record: in 1172 it was reckoned to have 13 parish churches, covering the much larger area then reckoned in the city.[1] Most other cities of these regions had a single parish, and a single parish church till the thirteenth century—though it was normal (unlike in Italy) for the parish church to be separate from the cathedral, and there were often monastic churches or communities of secular canons as well. Indeed it is common for the site of the parish church to reveal the history of the village community or communities before the town was formed. Thus Dijon had four (later five) parishes, because the town straddles the frontiers of four earlier, rural parishes. In south-western Germany, of 57 towns studied by Dr Müller in his paper on parish and town in this area, two-thirds had single parish churches outside their walls.[2] This reflected in most cases a parochial system laid down before the town; the church remained in the old village centre, and the town within its old parish. Where a church falls within the walls, it is even so sometimes on the edge of the medieval town; where it is in the centre, it is either because the town grew from an old village nucleus or because the town was planned so, was in fact one of Professor Beresford's new towns.[3] But in this area a parish church was evidently not felt to be an essential part of a new town or a new housing estate, so long as the old church was still within reasonable walking distance. To find more than one parish in a town is rare, and that again, as at Dijon, sometimes reflects a division more ancient than the town; sometimes peculiar local circumstances and factions.

Figures by themselves mean little; and the figures I have cited

---

[1] See W. Neuss and F. W. Oediger, *Das Bistum Köln*...(= *Geschichte des Erzbistums Köln*, vol. 1) (Köln 1964), pp. 282 ff., especially 286–7. There are several other good studies of the parishes in Cologne: see especially E. Hegel in *Die Kunstdenkmäler im Landesteil Nordrhein*, Beil. 2 (1950) and a brief account in G. Addleshaw, *The early Parochial system and the divine office* (London 1957).

[2] Ganshof, p. 49; Müller, 'Pfarrei und mittelalterliche Stadt'.

[3] Müller, 'Pfarrei und mittelalterliche Stadt', p. 76; for Beresford, see below, p. 73 n. 1.

can hardly be interpreted until we have defined what we mean by a parish and a parish church. But I quote these crude statistics at the outset to establish the extraordinary variety of the scene in Western Christendom in the eleventh and twelfth centuries.

There is, however, a fundamental ambiguity in any study of the proliferation of churches and parishes, and that is, obviously enough, that not every church was, or became, a parish church, and that parish boundaries evolved, and parish rights and responsibilities developed and altered.[1] From the twelfth century on, the canon lawyers hammered out a doctrine which has a certain simplicity: to your parish, to your parish church, and to your parish priest you owed attendance at Mass, you owed tithe; and to him and to it you delivered your children to be baptized, and they delivered you to be buried. Burial rights, baptismal rights, and tithe, on what we may with rough justice call a normal definition, though local varieties subsisted, were all essential to the making of a parish church; and that is why strict parochial boundaries of the kind familiar to us today can never have existed before the twelfth century; and much of the controversy that has raged from time to time about parochial origins has turned on these definitions. It was commonly assumed in many parts of Europe before the twelfth century that if you were a strong and healthy baby you went to the cathedral baptistery —or some suitable open space—to be baptized by the bishop on Easter Day or Whitsun; and it was commonly assumed or asserted that tithe should be paid to the mother church, not to the individual local village or town church where one worshipped. From the mother church, indeed, tithe was redistributed by the administrators of the welfare church; and that is why the most ancient parish boundaries in anything like our sense of the term are those, not of the parish churches, but of the diaconates of

[1] In general, see (for bibliography) H. Feine, *Kirchliche Rechtsgeschichte, Die katholische Kirche*, 4th ed. (Cologne–Graz 1964), pp. 411 ff.; Boyd, op. cit.; Kurze, op. cit. In earlier times the limitation was sometimes deliberate: as Professor Ullmann has pointed out to me, the decree of the Council of Tribur of 895, attempting to regulate the growth of parishes, should be stressed in this context (see the summary of ninth-century decrees on tithe and of the literature in Constable, pp. 40 ff.).

Rome.[1] Only when it became accepted that tithe was assessed on land, not on persons or on real or total income, and that it could legitimately be used—contrary to the practice of the early Church—for the support of the clergy, indeed mainly for the support of the clergy, could parish boundaries in a strict sense be established. Yet to refuse to employ the word 'parishes' for any institution earlier than 1100 would be absurd. Notoriously, *parochia* in early days more commonly meant a diocese (or any large area) than a parish; but it had been regularly used for a small unit of pastoral care long before the twelfth century, and many parishes had stable boundaries too, long before this era. I do not believe we shall make any sense of the word if we try to use any more precise definition than that a parish church was the place where the folk of a district worshipped regularly; to whose priest they looked for the sacraments, and whom they were expected, in some fairly direct sense, to support. In this sense the churches which sprang up in their thousands in the eleventh and twelfth centuries were clearly intended to be parish churches, whereas many of the oratories of the fourth, fifth or sixth centuries were not. One has only to compare the ecclesiastical map of London in the late Middle Ages with the earlier map of Poitiers as reconstructed by Dr Claude to see the force of this.[2] Poitiers had a continuity of religious life almost unique among the cities of north-western Europe; of this the fourth-century baptistery is still the outward symbol. In late Roman and early medieval times it proliferated churches. But these tended to spread in clusters around the cathedral within and the ancient house of St-Hilaire without the old city walls. In London in early days no doubt the churches were clustered, and the way St Gregory and St Augustine clung close to St Paul's in later

[1] See Boyd, pp. 47 ff., 129 ff. For the Roman 'Diaconiae', see esp. S. Kuttner in *Traditio*, III (1945), 178 ff.; cf. *Atlas of the Early Christian World*, ed. F. Van den Meer and C. Mohrmann (London 1959), map 27. For baptism by the bishop outside Italy, cf. Neuss and Oediger (p. 67 n. 1, p. 334) (Cologne); and below, p. 70 (Worcester). For what follows, see Constable (p. 64), chap. 1.

[2] For London see above, p. 66 n. 3; also the map of the *City of London showing Parish Boundaries Prior to...1907* printed by the London Topographical Society (1959), which in all essentials reflects the situation in 1200. For Poitiers see Claude, loc. cit. and *passim*, esp. pp. 36 ff.

times may well be a survival from such a time.[1] Nor did the final pattern closely resemble a chessboard or a chequer table. But a pattern there was in the end: the characteristic London parish was irregular in shape but fairly compact, covered about three and a half acres, and had at its centre a busy street, often a crossroads. The church has clearly been seen, from its inception, as the centre of a pastoral unit.

In theory churches grouped in this way could either be centres of separate pastoral units, as parish churches in the later sense, or outlying chapels of a minster or mother church, as St Helen's, Worcester, and its dependent chapels were viewed by Wulfstan's synod. One may find in different parts of Europe a wide variety of different stories, and in most the details elude us; but the development of the parochial system took place especially late, and so is comparatively well documented, in England, and I shall concentrate on the English evidence—not because it is typical, but because it shows with some clarity the forces at work. Orderic Vitalis was baptized in the little church at Atcham 'by the mighty river Severn': the nave walls which witnessed this ceremony in the 1070s substantially survive, though the font has long since gone;[2] but a glance at Francis Bond's *Fonts and Font Covers*[3] reveals how numerous are the Norman fonts which still bear witness that late eleventh- and twelfth-century churches were baptismal churches; and sufficient pre-Conquest fonts survive to show that this was no novelty, even though in the diocese of Worcester in the mid-eleventh century folk thronged to the cathedral with their babies to be received into the church at the hands of St Wulfstan, even before he became bishop.[4]

At the time of the Norman Conquest substantial traces of the organization of old minsters and mother churches still survived.[5]

[1] Cf. R. E. M. Wheeler, *London and the Saxons* (London Museum, 1935), esp. p. 100.
[2] On Atcham church, see H. M. and J. Taylor, *Anglo-Saxon Architecture* (Cambridge 1965), I, 30–2.
[3] London, 1908.
[4] *Vita Wulfstani* (p. 64), pp. 12–13; it is noted that he baptized the poor who could not afford to pay the normal fees.
[5] For what follows see F. Barlow, *The English Church 1000–1066* (London 1963), esp. pp. 179 ff., 183 ff. (with full references).

In most areas their pastoral office had long been substantially replaced by the local proprietary churches. In most areas the Normans rapidly obliterated the traces of the old organization by introducing the new pattern of archdeaconries and rural deaneries. Where the old pattern was persistent, as in the *parochia* of the old minster church at Leominster in Herefordshire, a curious conflict between old and new developed: Leominster was granted with all its rights to Reading Abbey by King Henry I; and these were deemed, as Dr Brian Kemp has shown, to include rights over all the churches of her ancient *parochia*;[1] indeed, the charters which confirm this grant list all the villages and hamlets of the neighbourhood, and one wonders if all the churches and chapels really existed, or whether some parts of the list are not an insurance against new churches which might be built in the future and so fall outside Reading's net. In any case, these confirmations are statements of pious hope rather than of established right; for in some cases at least Leominster's claim could not be upheld, since rights over churches of other kinds were established by rival landlords.

We see here an example of the fundamental confusion between spiritual and temporal rights, out of which the parish system was born. In the eleventh century a parish church was a piece of property; it could pass from father to son, it could be sold; it seems to have been freer than any other substantial piece of property from the shackles of local or feudal custom.[2] In his famous retort to Anselm, William Rufus likened his own relation to the greater abbeys to Anselm's relation to his manors: they were property from which one drew an income.[3] Churches, therefore, must have owners. Ancient churches were owned by bishops and cathedral chapters; some had long been owned by abbeys; a great number were owned by secular landlords who

---

[1] Dr Kemp's study of the Leominster complex is summarized in *EHR*, LXXXIII (1968), 505 ff.; more fully in his Reading Ph.D. thesis, 'The foundation of Reading Abbey and the growth of its possessions and privileges in England in the twelfth century' (1966).

[2] Feine (p. 68 n. 1), I, 129–78, esp. 139 ff. for bibliography; U. Stutz, *Geschichte des Kirchlichen Benefizialwesens...*, I (Berlin 1895, new ed. by H. E. Feine, 1961); for England, Barlow, pp. 186 ff. and 186 n. for references.

[3] Eadmer, *Historia Novorum*, ed. M. Rule (Rolls Series, 1884), pp. 49–50.

had built them or laid hands on them; a number more were owned by communities of burgesses. The burgesses of Norwich had 15 churches; one eminent burgess alone had $2\frac{1}{6}$.[1] Oddest of all, they could be owned by their priest; indeed, it seems fairly clear that, if the secular owner was lacking or had withdrawn into the background, it was assumed that the church must be owned by its priest. Thus Canterbury Cathedral Priory in the course of the eleventh century collected a little packet of London city churches, because their owners, the parish priests, had become monks at Canterbury and brought their churches with them.[2]

This curious situation had an economic and pastoral aspect. It is notorious that the confusion of spiritual and temporal property helped the growth of the parish system because it was in the interests of a lay owner to realize his assets by building a church and attracting tithe, of which in many cases he might easily be able to enjoy a considerable share. It represents a legal informality of a kind which must make the student of later parish history gasp. Broadly speaking, it was in the twelfth century that the canon law laid its cold hand on the parishes of Europe, and froze the pattern which has in many parts subsisted ever since. It is true that many new parishes have been formed, many amalgamated in the intervening centuries; that, for instance, the division of towns into a number of parishes characteristically took place in the twelfth century and later in Italy, and in the thirteenth century in the Low Countries.[3] But this was an orderly, organized process, not the free-for-all it had been in those cities which had been fragmented before the ice age. It depended on the co-operation of all the powers in the land; especially of bishop, king, lay patrons, and any religious house which was interested; and in any parish of much size or value, the Pope was commonly invited to help before the process was complete. In 1301 the Archbishop of York visited the king's new town, Kingston-upon-Hull, and found a funeral procession winding

[1] Barlow, p. 192.
[2] Ed. B. W. Kissan in *Trans. Middlesex Arch. Soc.*, new ser. VIII (1940), 57–69, cf. D. C. Douglas and G. W. Greenaway, *EHD*, II (London 1953), 954–6.
[3] See above, pp. 64 f. and nn.

along the Humber to a distant burial church, between a high tide and a gale; with a great effort he succeeded in arranging burial rights for the chapel of Holy Trinity, Hull; but this church, one of the greatest of medieval parish churches, was only truly made a parish church by Act of Parliament in 1661.[1] From 1200 to the mid-nineteenth century the whole of what is now Birkenhead—which included twelve hamlets—was the parish of Woodchurch, the wooden church which served them all; and eight hamlets in the north-west of the Wirral peninsula lay in the parish of West Kirby, the *by* with the church.[2] This is a pattern characteristic of the north-west, and of the northern marches of Wales. The most striking contrast is in London. By 1200 or so the parish boundaries were drawn; a few may have died in the later Middle Ages, but in all essentials the parishes survived—even when most of the churches were destroyed in the Great Fire and a majority disappeared altogether from view, until the Act of Parliament which redrew the boundaries in 1907.[3]

To a Londoner the period before 1200 seems the age of new parish churches *par excellence*; to a native of Florence or Utrecht, the twelfth or thirteenth century, to a sojourner in the Wirral peninsula, the nineteenth century would seem to be more truly such. These contrasts cannot be fully explained. The visitor to Florence, and to many other Italian cities, cannot fail to notice the Baptistery, outward and visible sign of the centuries when all the children of the city were brought to the Duomo to be baptized. If my theme was the dead rather than the living, a profitable hour might now be spent investigating the shifting sites of burial grounds. Within England, where the contrasts are most sharply defined, it is clear that one major factor which could check the escalation of parish churches was the presence of a large, powerful, and effective community of monks or canons in the town. For long periods in the tenth and eleventh centuries the sees of Worcester and York were held in plurality. It might therefore seem surprising that their ecclesiastical history

[1] M. W. Beresford, *New Towns of the Middle Ages* (London 1967), pp. 169 ff.
[2] G. Ormerod, *Hist. of the county Palatine and city of Chester*, 2nd ed. (by T. Helsby, London 1875–82), II, 485, 520.
[3] See above, pp. 66, 69.

in this period should be so different. A part at least of the explanation is that the bishop commonly resided with his community in Worcester; and that even after the Norman Conquest the first Norman Archbishop of York had great difficulty at first in scraping together a chapter of canons to serve his minster.[1] The community seems to have mattered more than the cathedral in such cases, and this is readily intelligible.

When the Norman bishops were settled firmly in the saddle, they showed by their actions contempt for the organization and the image of the old English hierarchy: they introduced archdeacons where few if any had lurked before; they redrew frontiers of lesser jurisdiction and established rural deaneries; they rebuilt all the cathedrals on a vast scale. When the clergy of the diocese of Canterbury led their folk to the cathedral in the 1080s in the Pentecostal procession, they entered a large new building whose open vista was dominated not by shrines or altars, but by the formidable figure of Archbishop Lanfranc, enthroned in the apse.[2] Whether the scorn which Lanfranc and his associates poured on their precursors was deserved has been widely doubted;[3] and no doubt rightly—but there is no question that the pre-Conquest Church was in many ways very different from its Norman successor. In particular, the incidence of a powerful religious community and an organizing bishop was much more sporadic than it later became.

If we plot the towns where parish churches multiplied, we may start in the north country, in York and Lincoln, cities free from communities of any stature before the very late eleventh century, cities which had lived in a pagan world a century before. At Norwich we are still in the Danelaw, though the southern Danelaw, and in a land where communities flourished. But

[1] So one may deduce from the telescoped narrative in Hugh the Chanter, *History of the Church of York*, ed. C. Johnson (Nelson's Med. Texts, 1967), p. 11; cf. *York Minster Fasti*, I, ed. Sir Charles Clay (Yorks Arch. Soc. Record Series, (CXXIII, 1958), pp. 1 ff.

[2] Cf. Brooke in *Bull. JRL*, L (1967), 23–4; *Collectanea Stephan Kuttner*, ed. G. Forchielli and A. M. Stickler, II = *Studia Gratiana*, XII (Bologna 1967), 42–3.

[3] Cf. esp. R. R. Darlington in *EHR*, LI (1936), 385 ff.; Barlow (p. 70 n. 5), *passim*.

Norwich itself had been the seat neither of a bishop nor of a religious community of consequence before the Conquest; and yet was one of the foremost English boroughs of the day. A complete catalogue would be tedious, indeed impossible in the present state of knowledge; but the briefest tour must take note of Canterbury, Winchester and London, for there the conditions were at first sight profoundly different. Canterbury never proliferated churches like York or Lincoln or London: yet Canterbury at the height had 22, and Winchester over twice that number; neither was a town of great size.[1] Neither was in the Danelaw; both had religious communities which one would have supposed powerful, both had rich bishops overseeing them. London has always been a law to itself. It is probable that the chapter of St Paul's was a small and comparatively insignificant affair before the Conquest;[2] and London had already earned something of that reputation for independence and power which was the hallmark of its history in the later Middle Ages.

To push an investigation of what the varieties of parish organization signify beyond this point is very difficult; in particular because we are in the dark as to the chronology of much church building. Five churches were dedicated to St Olaf in the city of London. They cannot have been dedicated to him before his death in July 1030; yet even in such a case we cannot be sure that one or more were not older churches rededicated. Nonetheless it would be unduly sceptical to leave nothing but cautions by way of explanation of so striking a phenomenon. It is clear that churches could multiply at any date; thus St Bride's, Fleet Street, and St Alban's, Wood Street, have long been supposed from their dedications to be comparatively early, and the spade has proved

---

[1] See above, p. 66 n. (Canterbury, York, Lincoln), 66 n., 69 n. (London). Mr Derek Keene is studying the Winchester churches, and kindly informs me that the number was about fifty by the late thirteenth century.

[2] The evidence is noted in *A History of St Paul's Cathedral*, ed. W. R. Matthews and W. M. Atkins (London 1957), pp. 13 ff., 18 ff., 361, 363; *Cambridge Hist. Journal*, x (1951), 111 ff.; M. Gibbs, introd. to *Early Charters of the Cathedral Church of St Paul, London* (Camden Third Series, LVIII (1939)). There was more continuity at St Paul's than elsewhere; even so the indications clearly are that it took a generation to build up the large Anglo-Norman chapter of the 1090s.

them so.[1] But it is also most unlikely that the escalation which produced a church for every three and a half acres came earlier than the eleventh century; and it was probably still in progress in the twelfth. In the case of York, Lincoln and Norwich it is really inconceivable that the medieval pattern of churches is older than the tenth and early eleventh centuries, since this area had to be reconverted in that period. It was reconverted to some purpose, however, and the evidence of surviving buildings and of Domesday Book combines to establish Lincolnshire as one of the parts of England most lavishly provided with parish churches before the Conquest.[2] The hypothesis that all these facts suggest is that in eleventh-century England numerous parish churches sprang up precociously where old institutions had grown weak or disappeared; and that the ecclesiastical geography and the personalities of the bishops in the eleventh century and especially in the mid-eleventh century (between the death of St Olaf and the death of Harold II), hold part of the key to our enigma. In York and Lincoln and Norwich one is in places where bishops held little sway in the century before the Conquest, and where old mother churches had long since disappeared. In York and Lincoln indeed there seems clearly to have been a revival, but at the parochial level mainly—though stirred no doubt by the distant patronage of Oswald and Wulfstan I, and later on by the wealth of Ealdred; or in Lincoln's case by the bishops who sat timorously at Dorchester peeping over the brink of their huge see.[3] In East Anglia the revival was in part monastic; but Bury and St Benet Hulme did not represent the

[1] On the cult of St Olaf, see B. Dickins in *Saga-Book of the Viking Society*, XII (1939), 53–80. On the excavations at St Bride's and St Alban's, Wood St. see W. F. Grimes, *The Excavation of Roman and Mediaeval London* (London 1968), pp. 182 ff., 203 ff. No such antiquity has been proved for St Swithun London Stone (ibid. pp. 199 ff.) which appears to be no older than the twelfth century. For an earlier study of these and similar dedications, see Wheeler (p. 70), pp. 100 ff.; cf. Brooke, *Time the archsatirist*, p. 20.

[2] Cf. W. Page, 'Some remarks on the Churches of the Domesday Survey', *Archaeologia*, LXVI (1915), 61–102, esp. 89, 92, with the indications in H. M. and J. Taylor, *Anglo-Saxon Architecture* (p. 70 n. 2).

[3] Cf. Barlow, pp. 215 ff., 227 ff., who gives, however, a somewhat more favourable picture of the diocese of York in particular than that suggested here.

activity of the Bishop of Elmham or Hoxne.[1] The see of East
Anglia has this in common with Canterbury and Winchester,
that in the mid-eleventh century it was in the hands of bishops
not noted for their pastoral zeal; first of Stigand, then of his
brother Æthelmær, bishops for nearly thirty years, and from
1052 to 1070 Stigand combined Winchester and Canterbury and
earned the reputation of serving neither.[2]

The church of St Olaf outside the gates of York was built by
Earl Siward, Macbeth's conqueror, in the mid-eleventh century;[3]
and there are many other cases known in which parish churches
were built by lesser and greater lords. It has sometimes been
assumed from this, and from the copious evidence that parish
churches were later the *Eigenkirchen* of manorial lords, that this
was the normal process. That is more than the evidence will
tell us, and within the towns it seems to me most unlikely. It is
really no more probable that the Earl of Leicester or his predecessors had built all the seven or so churches in the city which
he claimed to own than that they had been built by the city's
legendary founder, King Lear.[4] William Page in his book on
London's early history tried to align a number of baronial
'sokes' with later parish boundaries.[5] There is no reason to
suppose that any of the sokes within the walls were tidy geographical units, nor do we know the outline of any of them; so
that the enterprise is pure conjecture. What we do know is the
outline of the parishes, and in some cases, as Miss Honeybourne
has shown, we can be tolerably sure that the outline goes back
to the mid-eleventh century; though in others it must have
shifted much later than that.

[1] For the early sites of the bishopric of East Anglia see references in Brooke,
in *Studia Gratiana*, XII, 41 n. Bury was first established as an ecclesiastical centre
by Bishop Theodred of London in the first half of the tenth century (see
D. Whitelock, *Anglo-Saxon Wills* (Cambridge 1930), pp. 2 ff., 99 ff.); both
Bury and Hulme owed their first main endowment as monasteries to King
Cnut (see D. Knowles, *Monastic Order in England* (Cambridge 1940, and 2nd
edn. 1963), p. 70).
[2] Barlow, pp. 77 ff., gives a very fair judgement on Stigand.
[3] *VCH, York*, p. 397.
[4] On the parish churches of Leicester see *VCH, Leics.*, IV, 388–9.
[5] *London, its Origin and early Development* (London 1923), chap. IV, and pp. 159 ff.

I have suggested elsewhere that the churches of London were essentially, or largely, neighbourhood churches, like the churches of Norwich: that their site points not to the lord of a soke as their founder in most cases, but to a group of neighbours expressing a common piety.[1] Dedications to St Olaf and St Clement[2] may suggest that some of these groups consisted of communities from other parts of the world, though this can hardly be proved; but St Olaf at least hints at a link with the missionary world of Scandinavia. Professor R. B. Pugh has suggested to me that in some or many cases small town churches grew out of earlier crosses at street corners and crossroads, and in at least one case this is remarkably documented; that is the church of St James outside Micklegate at York, which Roger the priest (apparently of the early twelfth century) built where the cross had stood.[3] Their subsequent poverty, and the informality of their ownership, naturally followed if they represented the passing mood of piety of a group of neighbours; though the evidence from Norwich shows that the communities which built such churches could be kept in being for some generations; and in those towns which proliferated churches the proliferation continued into the twelfth and thirteenth centuries, suggesting a continuing interest in the movement. Such an interest on the Continent was in a number of cases enshrined in the practice of electing a parish priest. This practice can clearly be traced in many different parts of Europe in the early Middle Ages, as has been shown by Dr Kurze in his recent study of this obscure practice.[4] But he has also shown that evidence of it is rare in the twelfth and thirteenth centuries, and that most of the documented instances from the late Middle Ages reflect a new movement

[1] *Time the archsatirist*, pp. 20 ff. For Continental work on churches built by groups of merchants, see esp. Johansen (art. cit. pp. 64–5 n. 4); cf. also Kurze, pp. 308–9.

[2] Commonly reckoned a dedication characteristic of the Vikings (cf. St Clement Danes in London and the early dedications in Oslo: H. Christie in *Medieval Archaeology*, x (1966), 48).

[3] *Regesta Regum Anglo-Normannorum*, III, ed. H. A. Cronne and R. H. C. Davis (Oxford 1968), no. 987.

[4] For what follows see Kurze (p. 63 n. 3), *passim*.

towards popular participation in certain selected areas of Christendom. There is no decisive English evidence of parochial elections, but it is reasonable to suppose that it may well have been the practice in Norwich, and in other places where communal interest in neighbourhood churches survived.

All the evidence suggests that between priest and people in these tiny parishes there was an intimacy quite unusual in medieval pastoral relations. The Patarini in eleventh-century Milan attacked the Milanese clergy for secular vices—marriage and simony in particular; but the gravamen of their charges was that these folk were separated by their sins from the people at large.[1] In the long run the papal reform, where it succeeded most, separated clergy and people more than ever before, for it laid emphasis before all else on the view that layman and clerk, especially layman and priest, were clean different things. The renaissance of heresy in Milan two generations later has often been attributed to the failure of the Patarini: it could equally well be attributed to their success. If one judges that the separation of clergy and people was one of the most powerful factors in making some parts of Europe fertile soil for heresy in the twelfth century, then one may reckon the intimacy of clergy and people in English towns part of the explanation for the failure of heresy to take root in England in that period.[2] Part of the explanation: for we have here in view a complex phenomenon singularly ill documented. Nor do I wish to imply that ecclesiastical reform in the eleventh and twelfth centuries was in any simple sense damaging to pastoral success. It would be an absurd paradox to portray the clergy of the *Eigenkirchen* as models, the bishops and clergy of the new world as careless of lay concerns and lay opinion. There is a formidable body of evidence to the contrary, and the

[1] See C. Violante, *La pataria milanese e la riforma ecclesiastica*, I (Rome 1955); idem, 'I laici nel movimento patarino', *I Laici nella 'Societas Christiana' dei Secoli XI e XII* (Milan 1968), pp. 597–697; H. E. J. Cowdrey, 'The Papacy, the Patarenes, and the Church of Milan', *Trans. Roy. Hist. Soc.* 5th ser. XVIII (1968), 25–48.

[2] For the general problem see Brooke (1968), p. 60 n. 1; many aperçus on this problem are to be found in the proceedings of the 1965 conference at La Mendola on *I Laici* (above, n. 1).

thirteenth-century English bishops who instructed their clergy to instruct their people to provide baby-sitters when they went out in the evening were not wholly out of touch with the facts of secular life among married folk.[1]

The strength and weakness of the rank and file of the parish clergy in English towns is strikingly revealed in the document known as the *Law of the Northumbrian Priests*.[2] It presupposes that a group of priests of a fair size have been banded together into a sort of guild under the direction of the archbishop, and it has many clauses which emphasize the need for discipline and obedience to the archbishop. It is no coincidence that it survives in a collection linked with the most eminent reforming bishop of the early eleventh century, Wulfstan I of Worcester and York; and it seems probable that it represents an attempt by Wulfstan at the end of his life to instil discipline into the clergy of York. Simony and the sale of churches is forbidden, and so is bigamy; though it is presumed that a priest will have one 'woman'.[3] That they are parish clergy with baptismal rights seems presumed, a surprising concession from Wulfstan. The list of offences reflects a lively group of clergy, given to secular pleasures, such as brawling, drunkenness, and singing in taverns. No doubt it is a mistake to assume that every sin denounced by a medieval reformer was common practice; but parchment was expensive, Wulfstan in earnest, and the list is hardly likely to have been drawn up by haphazard.

There is no evidence of much of what constitutes pastoral work today, but what the document portrays is a lively group of clergy mingling with the crowd; with a sense of common purpose among themselves, but not separated from the folk among whom they worked by a different mode of life or excessive

[1] See the prolific synodal statutes in *Councils and Synods*, II, ed. F. M. Powicke and C. R. Cheney (Oxford 1964) esp. pt. I, 70, 444 and index, *s.v.* Children: safety measures for.

[2] F. Liebermann, *Gesetze der Angelsachsen* (Halle 1903–16), I, 380–5; translation and useful notes—including revision of Liebermann's date and evidence for Wulfstan's authorship or inspiration—by D. Whitelock in *EHD* (London 1955), I, 434–9.

[3] *c.* 35 (Whitelock, p. 437: cf. her note ad loc.).

education. This intimacy with the flock is emphasized by the design of parish churches in pre-Conquest and early Norman times. The characteristic little box with a shallow apse, small in a country church, often tiny in a town church, left no space for the celebrant to be separate from the people.[1] It is no coincidence that in the later twelfth and thirteenth centuries many chancels were rebuilt to allow more space; and in the fourteenth and fifteenth centuries these chancels became almost impenetrable boxes; the priests, men living in another world.[2] The open church of Norman times had as its true successor, not the divided parish church of the late middle ages, but the friars' churches. The friars devised their own architecture in the second generation of their existence, and its sources were complex.[3] Although the Franciscans have never forgotten that they started in the chapel of the Portiuncula, which is the tiniest of boxes, the characteristic hall-church—the large open space designed to suit the preacher and his audience rather than the celebration of the sacraments— was essentially a practical, functional solution to the clear needs of the friars as their work developed; and especially to their needs in northern countries whose climate is not always suited to preaching out of doors.

There is clearly a link between the forgotten parish clergy of the eleventh- and twelfth-century towns and the friars. The parish clergy were secular men, often no doubt with secular vices; they were worker priests, with the virtues and vices of their kind. They were readily accepted by their flocks as men of like passions, like St Francis's lay brothers; but the passions were so like, the assimilation sometimes so complete, that it might be wondered who was giving an example to whom. A grave misfortune overtook them in the papal reform; for its insistence on

[1] See esp. A. W. Clapham, *English Romanesque Architecture after the Conquest* (Oxford 1934), chap. VI and fig. 33; cf. H. M. and J. Taylor, *Anglo-Saxon Architecture, passim.*

[2] Cf. Brooke in *Bull. JRL*, L (1967), 13–33.

[3] Cf. esp. G. Meersseman, 'L'Architecture Dominicaine en XIIIe siècle, législation et pratique', *Archivum Fratrum Praedicatorum*, XVI (1946), 136–90; and (for England) A. R. Martin, *Franciscan Architecture in England* (Brit. Soc. of Franciscan Studies, 1937).

celibacy, on the superiority of the ascetic, monastic, regular life, made the rank and file parish clergy into second-class citizens.

It is easy to breed misunderstanding with a topic of this character. I am not delivering an attack on the papal reform. The abuses the reformers denounced were in many cases genuine abuses; the assimilation they abhorred often involved standards reminiscent of the whisky priests in Graham Greene's *The Power and the Glory*. The reformers thought they had found another way to convert the people, by setting up communities among them of ascetic clergy with pastoral responsibility. I do not wish now to enter discussion of the vexed question how much pastoral work monks and canons regularly undertook in this period.[1] In some cases clearly much; and one has only to read the *Life of St Wulfstan* or some of the miracle stories of the period to know that a saintly monk and a monastic community could form a pastoral centre of an effective kind. But there was certainly no 'policy' of monastic participation, and council after council of the early twelfth century denounced the practice; there is a curious tension between tithe regulations which presume that monks engage in pastoral work and conciliar decrees which deny that they shall.[2] This is one of the ways in which, in practice, pastoral work was frustrated by the activities of twelfth-century reformers. Nonetheless, it would be quite false to suppose that the missionary work of the clergy in the streets of Worcester or Cirencester or Gloucester, dominated by great religious communities, was necessarily less effective than in London or Norwich

[1] See M. Chibnall's statement of the literature and the issues in *JEH*, xviii 1967), 165–72, in which she charitably and reasonably takes me to task for some sentences in A. Morey and C. N. L. Brooke, *Gilbert Foliot and his letters* (Cambridge 1965), p. 85 and n., which may have given a misleading impression of the state of discussion of the topic. Among other points, she urges (p. 166) that insufficient attention has been paid in the recent literature to the distinction between temporal rights over churches and spiritual rights, and between serving the altar and serving the parish; this is a fair point, but it must be clearly understood that many folk failed to see the first distinction in the late eleventh and early twelfth centuries, and that the nature of 'parish work' in this period is exceedingly obscure. Mrs Chibnall's article contains valuable evidence on several of the topics discussed here, especially on the definition of a parish.

[2] See Constable (p. 64 n. 1), chap. ii, pp. 136 ff. (esp. p. 144), 165 ff.

or Lincoln. But it was different, and these towns had opportunities denied to the others.

The parish church in London was a tiny centre for a small community; a local cult centre. St Paul might preside on his hill in the west end of the city, as Thor and Othen presided in the Scandinavian Olympus; but the centre of the religious world for ordinary folk was the small relic, the small stone, the small cross, and the little church which they had built. Into their religion we can hardly penetrate; but certain things we can state with confidence. To build a hundred churches in a space no larger than 350 acres presupposes a degree of sustained devotion unusual in the history of the Church—devotion no doubt to other things as well as to God; for St Olaf may represent the loyalties of an alien community and a parish pump, even a status symbol of a modest kind; and as a missionary, Olaf himself had represented the view that conversion should be by force and fraud, if other methods failed. But the central interest, as I see it, of this escalation of churches is that it shows a popular religious movement in its natural setting—it shows what happened if the folk were left to develop their cultus according to their own devices—and the power in a broad sense of a spontaneous missionary endeavour. In the thirteenth century St Francis tried in a modified way to revive the idea of conversion by infiltration and example, and his original inspiration suffered the same fate as the humble, obscure, but undoubtedly effective work of the parish clergy of the eleventh and twelfth centuries.

By the kindness of Professor J. Kloczowski and Dr E. Wisniowski I am able to add references to a recent study of parish structure in Poland, which will help future students of this subject to spread this kind of parochial investigation more widely in a fruitful way.[1]

---

[1] E. Wisniowski, Rozwoj organizacji parafialnej w Polsce du czasów Reformacji (Development of parochial structures in Poland to the Reformation), in: *Kościòt w Polsci I* (= Église en Pologne, vol. 1, ed. J. Kloczowski), Kraków, 1968, pp. 239 ff. (summary and bibliography).

THE PROBLEM OF THE NATIVE CLERGY IN THE PORTUGUESE AND SPANISH EMPIRES FROM THE SIXTEENTH TO THE EIGHTEENTH CENTURIES

by C. R. BOXER

A LEARNED Jesuit historian of the Japan mission recently observed: 'The aim of Christian missionary activity in every mission land is to establish the Church. The goal of the foreign missionary is primarily to prepare the ground and lay the foundation of the future Church. What he envisages, therefore, is the idea of a fully matured hierarchy of native-born bishops and priests capable of carrying on the work of the Church without foreign assistance.'[1]

Identical sentiments have been voiced by other erudite Jesuit historians of Portuguese India and the Spanish Philippines; but their own well-documented works show very clearly that, however much this was a consummation devoutly to be wished, the road to its achievement was a long and an arduous one. Indeed, at times this objective was actively opposed by those very missionaries who should have been most anxious to attain it. Whatever the theory may have been, in practice the indigenous clergy were apt to be kept in a strictly subordinate condition to the European priests, particularly where these latter were members of the Regular clergy. How this discrimination arose, and the length of time for which it endured, is the theme of this paper.

As a result of the Portuguese voyages of discovery round the African coast and the opening of the sea-route to India, a number of West Africans had been taken to Lisbon, where some of them received a religious training and education. Very few of them

---

[1] Hubert Cieslik, S.J., 'The Training of a Japanese Clergy in the Seventeenth Century', p. 41 of the reprint from J. Ruggendorf, S.J. (ed.), *Studies in Japanese Culture* (Tokyo 1963).

seem to have returned to their respective homelands as priests or as catechists; although one who did so was a Lisbon-educated Congolese ordained as titular Bishop of Utica in 1518, at the insistence of King Manuel of Portugal. This precedent of a Negro bishop was not followed for several centuries; but a papal brief dated 12 June of the same year authorized the royal chaplain at Lisbon to ordain 'Ethiopians, Indians, and Africans' who might reach the moral and educational standards required for the priesthood. The first step was thus taken towards the formation of a native clergy, but a good many years elapsed before matters proceeded much further. The projected evangelization of the old Kingdom of Congo foundered after a promising start, largely owing to the greater attractions of the West African slave trade, and to the tropical diseases which decimated the missionary personnel and militated against continuity of effort.

For the first four decades of the sixteenth century the only religious Order represented in Asia was the Franciscan. These Friars Minor, and the relatively few Portuguese secular clergy in India, had more than enough to do in ministering to their own countrymen in the East. The strength of the Indian caste-system and their own ignorance of the Hindu religion and of Indian languages for long prevented them from making more than a few converts, other than among Asian women who had married Portuguese men, and their household slaves, servants, and dependants. For these and other reasons, the Portuguese made no attempt to form an indigenous clergy in India before the year 1541. The very few Indians who were ordained as secular priests during this period were not converts from Hinduism, but 'St Thomas Christians' of the Syrian–Chaldean rite, about 300,000 of whom lived on the Malabar coast of south-west India, ministered to by priests owing obedience to their patriarch in Mesopotamia. Between 1510 and 1661 only half a dozen Indians seem to have been admitted into the Franciscan Order, and three of these had been ordained not by the Portuguese prelates in India but at Rome.

In 1532 Frei Rodrigo de Serpa, the Franciscan commissary at Goa, complained to the king that his Superiors in Portugal had refused to allow him to accept novices in India, promising that they would always send enough friars from Portugal each year to fill the gaps caused by death and disease. This, however, they had failed to do; and Fr Rodrigo had accordingly admitted not only some Portuguese laymen serving in India, but some half-castes or *mestiços* who had been born there—sons of Portuguese fathers and Indian mothers. He urged the king to obtain his Superiors' approval for this step, claiming that these *mestiços* were almost as good as European-born Portuguese. He also pointed out that it was more economical to recruit novices locally than to have them sent by the long, dangerous and expensive voyage from Lisbon to Goa. He further argued that the unconverted Indian relations on the *mestiço*'s mother's side would be more likely to become converted in this way, while the Portuguese fathers were greatly scandalized at the Franciscans' refusal to accept their Eurasian sons. Fr Rodrigo did not envisage the creation of a specifically Indian clergy, but only the admission of carefully selected half-castes; but even this limited concession was regarded askance in Portugal.[1]

The first serious attempt to undertake the formation of a native clergy in Portuguese Asia dates from 1541. In that year the vicar-general of Goa, Miguel Vaz, persuaded the local civil and ecclesiastical authorities to sponsor the foundation of a Seminary of the Holy Faith (Santa Fé) for the religious education and training of Asian and East African youths, neither Europeans nor Eurasians being admitted. A few years later this institution was taken over by the Jesuits, who had just arrived in India, and it was attached to their College of St Paul at Goa. They allowed the admission of a few European and Eurasian youths, though basically this establishment continued to be a seminary for the training of Asian catechists and secular priests, who were destined to work in the mission-fields between the Cape of Good Hope and Japan. In 1556 there were 111 pupils at this seminary, composed of the following nationalities: 19 European-born Portuguese; 10 *castiços*, or boys born of white Portuguese parents in

---

[1] Fr. Rodrigo de Serpa, O.F.M., to the Crown, Goa, 8 November 1532, in A. da Silva Rego (ed.), *Documentação para a história das missões do Padroado Portugûes do Oriente. Índia* (12 vols. Lisbon 1947–58), II, 213–15.

Asia; 15 *mestiços*, or Eurasians; 13 'Malabares', who were probably St Thomas Christians; 21 *Canarins*, or Marathi–Konkani inhabitants of Goa; 5 Chinese; 5 Bengalis; 2 Peguans; 3 'Kaffirs' or Bantu from East Africa; 1 Gujarati; 1 Armenian; 5 'Moors', or ex-Muslims; 6 Abyssinians; and 5 boys from the Deccan sultanates. It was thus an inter-racial institution in the fullest sense of the term. The age of admission was fixed at not less than 13 and not more than 15 years. The curriculum was closely modelled on that of the Jesuit colleges in Europe, with Latin and theological studies predominating. But the students had to practise their own vernaculars in their respective national groupings twice daily, so that they would retain fluency in their native tongues. Those who graduated were eligible to be ordained as secular priests, but not before attaining the age of 25 if they were non-Europeans.[1]

As might have been expected, there were sharp differences of opinion among the Portuguese in India over the character and the potentialities of these indigenous students in their early years. A few of the Jesuit missionaries themselves were frankly hostile to, or at least very sceptical about, the whole experiment. These critics shared the widely held view which was later epitomized by Hilaire Belloc with his aphorism: 'The Faith is Europe, and Europe is the Faith'. One of the early rectors, Padre António Gomes, stated frankly: 'The people of this land are for the most part poor-spirited, and without Portuguese priests we will achieve nothing. For the Portuguese laymen here will not go to confession with an Indian or with a Eurasian priest, but only with a pure-bred Portuguese.' Even that ardent missionary St Francis Xavier, who warmly supported and re-organized the seminary and the contiguous College of St Paul, did not envisage that the Indian trainees would make more than good catechists, auxiliaries and, at the most, secular priests. He did not advocate that Indian aspirants should be admitted to the

[1] 'Rol dos Alunos do Colegio de Goa', November 1556, in Silva Rego, *Documentação. Índia*, VI, 101–6. Cf. also C. Merces de Melo, S.J., *The Recruitment and Formation of the Native Clergy in India, 16th–19th Centuries: an Historico-Canonical study* (Lisboa 1955), pp. 65–85.

Society of Jesus itself. Some of the St Thomas Christians who had been ordained by the pioneer Franciscans did not turn out well. Some of the pupils in the Jesuit College of St Paul could not last the exacting course, where the medium of instruction was in Latin. These disappointments, inevitable though they were in first- or second-generation Christians, together with the open contempt expressed by the Portuguese laymen for Indian and Eurasian priests, led to a hardening of the attitudes of all the religious Orders. A Jesuit Visitor at Goa wrote to the General of the Society at Rome in December 1568:

Experience has taught us that it is not now convenient for us to admit the natives of the land into the Society, not even if they are *mestiços*. The Superiors of the other religious Orders have likewise come round strongly to this way of thinking. Withal, I personally feel that if they are well trained and indoctrinated, some of them may be able to help the Ordinary. And in course of time, we may even be able to admit a very few of them ourselves, so as not to close the door altogether against any nation, since Christ Our Lord died for us all.[1]

In point of fact, only one Indian was ordained a priest in the Society of Jesus, a Christian Brahmin named Pero Luís, who was ordained in 1575. Although he proved to be an excellent priest, who warmly pleaded for the admission of a few of his compatriots just before his death in 1596, the fourth Jesuit General, Everard Mercurian, had firmly closed the door against the admission of Asians and Eurasians in 1579.[2] An exception was soon made in favour of the Japanese, and this favour was later extended successively to Chinese, Vietnamese, and Koreans; but the ban on the admission of Indians was retained until the suppression of the Society of Jesus in the Portuguese empire in 1760. Sooner or later, all the other religious Orders working in the East adopted the precedent set by the Jesuits. For instance, the Franciscans, who in 1589 were still admitting *mestiços* as

[1] Padre-Visitador Gonçalo Álvares, S.J., to the Jesuit General Francisco Borgia, Goa, Dec. 1568, in Josef Wicki, S.J., *Documenta Indica*, VII, 575.
[2] J. Wicki, S.J.,'Pedro Luis Brahmane und erster indischer Jesuit', in *Neue Zeitschrift für Missionswissenschaft*, VI (1950), 115–26; Mercurian's letter of 1579 to the Jesuit Provincial at Goa is printed in C. Merces de Melo, S.J., *Native Clergy*, p. 166 n.

novices at Goa (though they had been ordered not to do so by their Superiors in Portugal), fifty years later were priding themselves on the fact that they had a rigidly exclusive colour-bar. They even sent a special emissary to Lisbon, Madrid and Rome to assure the king and the Pope that they only admitted novices of pure white race, including those whose parents were born in India.[1]

What happened in Portuguese Asia was closely paralleled by developments in Spanish America and in the Philippines. Indeed, it is very likely that the Spanish-American precedents in implementing a rigid colour-bar in the colonial Church influenced Everard Mercurian's decision to reject Indians and Eurasians in 1579. As with the Portuguese, the religious Orders working in the Spanish colonial empire originally had no colour-bar in their respective constitutions, but by the end of the sixteenth-century they had a very rigid one. In 1525 a certain Rodrigo de Albornoz advised the Crown of Castile from Mexico:

In order that the sons of the caciques and [native] lords be instructed in the Faith, Your Majesty must needs command that a College be founded wherein they may be taught reading, grammar, philosophy, and other arts, to the end that they may be ordained priests; for he who shall become such among them will be of greater profit in attracting others to the Faith than will fifty [European] Christians.[2]

This and similar suggestions for the formation of an Amerindian clergy induced the Crown to found the College of Santiago Tlateloco, which was inaugurated in 1536 and entrusted to the management of the Franciscans. The pupils were limited to the sons of the indigenous Mexican aristocracy; and the college was expected to serve the dual purpose of forming a cultural élite among the laity and providing a certain number of native priests. The experiment was not a success; and its failure led to the ecclesiastical synods and councils which were celebrated in

---

[1] Fr. Miguel da Purificação, O.F.M., *Relação Defensiva dos filhos da India Oriental, e da Provincia do Apostolo S. Thomé dos frades menores da regular observancia da mesma India* (Barcelona 1640).

[2] In Constantine Bayle, S.J., 'España y el clero indígena de America', in *Razon y Fé*, XCIV (1931), 216.

Mexico and Peru during the second half of the sixteenth century passing drastic measures intended to prevent the formation of an indigenous clergy. The first Council of Mexico (1555) declared that holy orders were not to be conferred on Amerindians, *Mestizos* and mulattoes, who were classed with the descendants of Muslims and of persons sentenced by the Inquisition as inherently lacking the good repute which befitted the sacerdotal character. The third Council of Mexico eased this prohibition slightly in 1585; but it also enacted that 'Mexicans who are descended in the first degree from Amerindians, or from Moors, or from parents of whom one is a Negro, must not be admitted to holy orders without great care being exercised in their selection'. The second Council of Lima (1591) renewed the blanket-prohibition of 1555 by decreeing *tout court* that 'Amerindians are not to receive any of the Orders of the Church'. As regards *Mestizos*, the ecclesiastical policy finally adopted was somewhat more liberal, their right to ordination being expressly decreed by the Crown of Castile in 1588, provided they were 'well educated, properly qualified, and born legitimately in wedlock'. But the policy of both Church and State was to limit the number of Mestizo clergy as far as possible, preference being given to the ordination of Creoles (men born of pure white parents in the colonies) and, in the higher ranks of the clergy above all, to peninsula-born Spaniards. The restrictions on Negroes and mulattoes were always rigidly maintained. Never did they rise in the social scale, and they were never admitted to any ecclesiastical Orders in Spanish America and the Philippines, unless, perchance, they could pass themselves off as *Mestizos*.[1]

The advocates of the formation of a native clergy who, though relatively few and far between, did exist, argued that since Jews and Gentiles who were newly converted to the Faith in the primitive Church had been ordained as priests and even promoted to bishops, the same privilege should be extended to the sons of converted Amerindians. 'For these men know the native languages better and could preach and minister more acceptably in them.

[1] C. S. Braden, *Religious Aspects of the Conquest of Mexico* (Duke University Press 1930), pp. 270–7.

Moreover, the people would then receive the Gospel at the lips of their own brothers more freely than from foreigners.' A leading Franciscan missionary-friar of great experience in Mexico, Fr Geronimo de Mendieta (1538–1604), rebutted these arguments as follows in his *Historia Eclesiástica de las Indias*:

To this problem, it will be enough to reply by admitting that in the primitive church it was thus, and that it was fitting then, for God worked by miracles on the new converts and they became saints and even martyrs to the name of Jesus. But in these times, the Church, illumined by the Holy Spirit, and taught by the experience which it has had of the many backslidings among the new Christians, has ordained that by determination of the high priests, the vicars of Christ, that there shall not be admitted to the profession of priesthood or the Orders, the descendants of any infidel in the fourth degree, and this is especially provided in the constitution of the Franciscan Order. But I would add further that, even providing that they would not return to the vomit of their heathen rites and ceremonies (which is the reason why the Church deprives them of this privilege), there exists among them a greater cause than in other descendants of infidels why they should not be admitted even as lay-brothers, namely, that the majority of them are not fitted to command or rule, but to be commanded and ruled. I mean to say that they are not fitted for masters but for pupils, not for prelates but for subjects, and as such they are the best in the world. So good are they in this respect, that even I, poor and weak as I am, with only the backing and favour of the king, I could with little aid from any companions have a province of 50,000 Amerindians so well ordered and Christian that it would seem to be a monastery.[1]

This ecclesiastical policy of racial discrimination was naturally extended to the Philippines after the Spanish occupation and Christianization of most of that island group in the second half of the sixteenth century. Fr Diego Aduarte, a Dominican missionary-friar with great experience in the Far Eastern mission-field, who became Bishop of Nueva Segovia in 1632, strongly opposed the attempt of his colleague, Fr Diego Collado, O.P., to found a religious congregation which would accept Filipino vocations

---

[1] In C. S. Braden, *Religious Aspects*, p. 272.

for missionary priests. Aduarte wrote of this scheme, that 'it was something not worth considering…[and] it ran counter to the views of all intelligent persons who had ever been in the Indies, and against everything that experience had shown, ever since the religious Orders had worked therein'.[1] Similarly, when Sebastian Hurtado de Corcuera, the Governor-General of the Philippines, founded the Seminary of San Felipe de Austria at Manila in 1641, rule 3 of the regulations for this institution stipulated that: 'the collegiates must be of pure [white] race and have no mixture of Jewish or Moorish blood to the fourth degree; and they shall have no Negro or Bengali blood, or that of any similar nation in their veins, or a fourth part of Filipino blood'.[2] As with the Portuguese in Asia, however, the Spanish religious Orders working in the Philippines made an exception in favour of admitting Japanese as lay-brothers and even, on rare occasions, as priests, until the Japan mission was extinguished in blood by the persecution of the Tokugawa Shoguns in 1640.

Another reason for the maintenance of a rigid colour-bar in the colonial Church and State of the two Iberian empires which, it will be recalled, formed a dual monarchy and empire under the Spanish branch of the House of Habsburg from 1580 to 1640, was provided by the Portuguese *Padroado* and the Castilian *Patronato* (*Patronazgo*) *Real*. Diogo do Couto, a Portuguese soldier-chronicler who spent most of his life in India, observed in 1612: 'The kings of Portugal always aimed in their conquest of the East at so uniting the two powers, spiritual and temporal, that the one should never be exercised without the other.'[3] This indissoluble union of the Cross and the Crown was exemplified in the exercise of the *Padroado Real*, or royal patronage of the Church, which can be loosely defined as a combination of the rights and duties inherited by the Crown of Portugal since the middle of the fifteenth century as patron of the Roman Catholic

---

[1] Fr Diego Aduarte, O.P., *Historia de la Provincia del Santo Rosario de la Orden de Predicadores en Philippinas, Iapon, y China* (Manila 1640), II, cap. 51.

[2] Horacio de la Costa, S.J., 'The Development of the Native Clergy in the Philippines', in *Theological Studies*, VIII (June 1947), 228.

[3] Diogo do Couto, *Decada VI* (Lisbon 1612), IV, chap 7.

missions and ecclesiastical establishments successively in Africa, in Asia, and in Brazil. In fact, the Portuguese *Padroado Real* in the non-European world was only limited by the similar papal privileges conferred on the Castilian kings' *Patronato Real* in Spanish America and the Philippines from the time of Columbus onwards. The Renaissance popes, owing to their preoccupation with European politics, with the rising tide of Protestantism, and with the Turkish threat to the Holy Roman Empire and to Italy, did not concern themselves closely with the evangelization of the new worlds opened by the Spanish and Portuguese discoveries. These popes saw no harm in letting the two Iberian Crowns bear the expense of building chapels and churches, maintaining a colonial religious hierarchy, and sending missionaries to convert the heathen, in exchange for granting those two Crowns extensive privileges in the way of presenting bishops to vacant colonial sees, collecting tithes, and administering ecclesiastical taxation. The king of Portugal (in his capacity of governor and admini-strator of the Order of Christ) was the patron in his colonial empire, and the king of Spain (in his capacity of king of Castile) in his. Their respective colonial representatives, the viceroys and governors, acted as vice-patrons, enforcing the royal will in ecclesiastical affairs. No papal brief, bull, or document emanating from Rome was regarded as valid in the two Iberian colonial empires until it had been endorsed and registered in the respective royal chancery, whether at Lisbon or Madrid. The two Crowns controlled the movements of all the missionary and ecclesiastical personnel to and from their respective Indies. The *Padroado* and the *Patronato* were among the most jealously guarded regalia of these two Crowns. Appeals from their respective jurisdictions to that of Rome, though theoretically possible, were made extremely difficult in practice if either Crown wished to obstruct such a course. Naturally enough, the kings of Portugal and Spain strove to fill most of the higher ecclesiastical posts in their overseas territories with peninsula-born clergy. They also strove to keep a close control over the missionaries and members of the religious Orders by ensuring that their Superiors should be of the same origin, or at any rate individuals of proved loyalty.

The *Padroado* and the *Patronato* thus presented two further and highly effective barriers to the formation of a fully fledged native clergy complete with its own hierarchy.[1]

By the mid-seventeenth century the attitude of the papacy had changed considerably. Successive popes had found that the extensive privileges, amounting to a monopoly of ecclesiastical patronage, which had been so freely bestowed on the Crowns of Portugal and Castile in the two previous centuries, were in many respects highly inconvenient and subversive of papal authority. There was very little that the papacy could do about the Spanish-American empire, where the Castilian Crown's *Patronato Real* was maintained intact—indeed in some respects it was strengthened during the eighteenth century—down to the wars of independence in the early nineteenth century. But the Portuguese Crown was in a much weaker position after its monopoly of the Asian and African seas had been broken by the Dutch and the English in 1600. The papacy was therefore enabled to whittle down and pare away the claims of the Portuguese *Padroado Real* in both Asia and Africa throughout the seventeenth and eighteenth centuries. This increasing papal control of the missions was exercised primarily through the Sacred College of the *Propaganda Fide*, founded at Rome in 1622, and secondarily through papal encouragement of French and Italian missionary enterprises in Africa and in the East. In Brazil it was another story. The Portuguese position on the other side of the Atlantic was as strong as that of the Spaniards in the rest of Latin America; and the papacy was constrained to admit the full functioning of the Portuguese *Padroado* in Brazil until that country achieved her independence in 1825.

If we take a rapid survey of the position of the native clergy in the mid-seventeenth century, we find something like the following situation. The oldest of the West African colonies, the Cape Verde Islands, were described by their Portguese governor in 1627 as being 'the dung-heap' of the Portuguese empire; but

---

[1] For a comparison of the Goan and Filipino native clergy in this respect, see J. H. da Cunha Rivara, 'As Parochias do Ultramar disputadas entre o clero secular e o regular', in *Chronista de Tissuary*, I (Nova Goa 1866), 137–44.

twenty-five years later, no less a person than the celebrated Padre António Vieira, S.J., penned a glowing eulogy of the local dean and chapter. 'They are all black', he wrote from Santiago de Cabo Verde on Christmas Day 1652, 'but it is only in this respect that they differ from Europeans...There are here clergy and canons as black as jet, but so well bred, so authoritative, so learned, such great musicians, so discreet and so accomplished, that they may be envied by those in our own cathedrals at home.'[1] As in Cape Verde, the bulk of the clergy in the islands of São Tomé and Príncipe were composed of mulattoes and free Negroes, since their indigenous blood gave them a better resistance to tropical diseases, and the white clergy were loath to leave Portugal for a region which had quickly earned the sobriquet of the 'white man's grave'. There was a longstanding rivalry between the black and the mulatto clergy of São Tomé, which sometimes culminated in armed clashes; nor could a high standard of conduct normally be expected in such remote outposts, which were often without a resident bishop for long periods. Along the Guinea Coast of West Africa in its widest sense, from the mouth of the Senegal River to that of the Congo, which had been frequented by the Portuguese for some two centuries, no native clergy had been formed, nor was the formation of one really practicable. The old Kingdom of Congo, on the other hand, whose core was in the region now known as northern Angola, had been superficially Christianized in the reign of the King Dom Afonso I (1506–43). A century later, this kingdom was still nominally Christian, at least in part, and there were a few mulatto and Negro priests in the capital of São Salvador; but their quality usually left much to be desired, according to the few Jesuit and Capuchin missionaries who sometimes made their way there. Similar criticisms were levied against the mulatto secular clergy in Angola, particularly by the Italian Capuchin missionary-friars who worked in this region from 1649 onwards. But the annual death-rate among the white clergy, whether secular or Regular, was so high that the services of the much-criticized but better-

[1] Letter of António Vieira, S.J., Santiago do Cabo Verde, 25 December 1652, in J. L. d'Azevedo (ed.), *Cartas do Padre António Vieira S.J.*, I, 295.

acclimatized mulatto clergy could not be dispensed with, as the Bishop of Congo and Angola pointed out in 1689.[1]

The relative frequency with which mulattoes and (less often) Negroes were ordained as priests in some parts of Portuguese West Africa, contrasts curiously with the complete want of an indigenous clergy in the Portuguese possessions on the East African coast from the time of Vasco da Gama to the present day, Seminaries of a sort, however inferior, were established during the sixteenth and seventeenth centuries for the education of an indigenous clergy in the Cape Verde Islands, São Tomé, and Luanda (Angola). But not until 1761 did the Lisbon government order the foundation of a seminary at Moçambique island for the same purpose on the east coast. The terms of this decree expressly envisaged the ordination of mulattoes and free Negroes as well as of whites, quoting the historical and canonical precedent of the 'kingdom of Angola and the islands of São Tomé and Príncipe, where the parish priests, canons, and other dignitaries are usually the black clergy who are natives of that region'.[2] Although this measure was originated by that dreaded dictator of Portugal, who is best known by his later title of Marquis of Pombal, it was not implemented in East Africa until over two hundred years later. It is true that some Bantu of East African origin were ordained at Goa in the seventeenth and eighteenth centuries, including a brother of the paramount chief of the tribal confederacy of Monomotapa in East Central Africa. Fr Antonio Ardizone Spinola, an Italian Theatine missionary who knew this Negro Dominican friar at Goa, reported that, although 'he is a model priest, leading a very exemplary life and saying Mass daily, yet not even the habit which he wears secures him any consideration whatever in this place, just because he has a black face. If I had not seen it, I would not have believed it'. Fr Antonio Ardizone was a highly vocal critic of the Portuguese maintenance of a rigid colour-bar in Church and State, as he showed during a series of outspoken sermons on this theme

[1] Bishop's letter, Luanda, 25 February 1689, in Louis Jadin, *Le Congo et la secte des Antoniens, 1694–1718* (Brussels 1961), p. 430.
[2] In A. A. de Andrade, *Relações de Moçambique Setecentista* (Lisbon 1955), pp. 599–601.

which he preached during his stay at Goa in 1639–48, and at Lisbon after his return to Europe, but not all of his clerical colleagues agreed with him.[1] Another Italian Theatine, Fr Pietro Avitabile, who worked at Goa during the same period, while recommending the local Indian secular clergy to the good graces of the cardinals of the *Propaganda Fide* at Rome, added significantly: 'None of the religious Orders here allows these natives to take their holy habit. At first I thought that this was very blameworthy; but experience has made me feel that their refusal is fully justified.'[2] Moreover, the few Bantu priests from Moçambique who were ordained at Goa were not sent back to East Africa to work among their own people there, but they were retained for use in Portuguese India. The coloured clergy and friars of Moçambique, who were the target of so much criticism by governors and Crown officials in the eighteenth century, were exclusively Goans or Indo-Portuguese by origin.

In Portuguese India itself the native secular clergy, which was recruited from the *Canarins* or sons of the soil, and educated at the Seminary of Santa Fé, or by one or another of the religious Orders from 1550 onwards, was kept in a strictly subordinate position to the European-born Regular clergy for over two centuries. The Indian secular priests were merely used as auxiliaries to the European Regulars, who likewise provided most of the parish priests, even when the inhabitants of Goa and the adjacent islands had been devout and faithful Christians for several generations. Moreover, these indigenous secular priests were recruited from the highest castes only; that is to say from the Brahmins (or *Brahmenes* as the Portuguese called them) and occasionally from the *Khsatriyas* or Warrior caste. The Indian Christians kept and indeed still retain their caste divisions, in spite of their conversion to Christianity. Yet the Portuguese ecclesiastical and secular authorities did not trust them, and some of the archbishops of Goa were singularly reluctant to ordain any Indians at all. One of these prelates, D. Christovão de Sá e

---

[1] Fr Antonio Ardizone Spinola, O.C.R.Th., *Cordel Triplicado de Amor a Christo Jesu sacramentado lançado em tres livros de Sermoens* (Lisbon 1680).

[2] Letter of Fr Pietro Avitabile, O.C.R.Th., Goa, 31 December 1645, in C. Merces de Melo, S.J., *Native Clergy in India*, 247–8.

Lisboa (1610–22), is said to have sworn on the missal never to do so. The first breach in the theory and practice of white superiority in the ecclesiastical hierarchy of Portuguese India was effected when the Christian Brahmin, Matheus de Castro, after being refused ordination by the Archbishop of Goa, made his way overland in 1625 to Rome. Here he was not only ordained a priest but, after completing his theological studies with great credit, he was consecrated Bishop of Chrysopolis *in partibus infidelium*, and subsequently appointed vicar-apostolic of Bijapur. But although he was warmly supported by the Congregation of the *Propaganda Fide* at Rome, the Portuguese authorities at Goa refused to allow him to function on their territory, claiming that the papal documents which he carried had been obtained under false pretences. His principal critic was the venerable Jesuit patriarch of Ethiopia, Dom Afonso Mendes, who did not scruple to term his colleague of Chrysopolis 'a bare-bottomed Nigger'.[1] The mutual denunciations of these two prelates reminds one of Cunninghame Graham's jocose remark concerning the controversy between the Jesuits and Bishop Cardenas which raged in Paraguay during the mid-seventeenth century: 'Hell has been said to have no fury equal to that of a woman scorned, but a bishop thwarted makes a very tolerable show.'[2]

If the secular Canarim clergy at Goa and elsewhere in Portuguese India was still kept in a rigorously subordinate and inferior position by the European-born ecclesiastical hierarchy, at least this indigenous clergy was fairly numerous and firmly established. This was more than could be said for the regions under the sway of the Castilian Crown's *Patronato*, where an indigenous clergy of any kind did not yet exist. We have seen that projects for the formation of a native clergy were mooted from time to time, but they either remained on paper, or else they were speedily aborted. The general attitude of the Spanish colonial hierarchy to this problem was exemplified by Archbishop Pardo of the Philippines in the last quarter of the seventeenth century.

---

[1] Theodore Ghesquière, *Mathieu de Castro, premier vicaire apostolique aux Indes* (Louvain 1937), p. 32; Merces de Melo, S.J., *Native Clergy in India*, 215–26.

[2] R. B. Cunninghame Graham, *A Vanished Arcadia* (ed. 1901), p. 121.

When consulted by the Crown about the possibility of training and forming an indigenous Filipino clergy, the archbishop reacted with a markedly unfavourable opinion in the year 1680. He claimed that the Filipinos had little or no inclination for theological studies and moral philosophy. There was also the additional handicap of what he stigmatized as their evil customs, their natural vices, and their preconceived ideas. All these factors made it necessary to treat them as if they were children, even when they were fifty or sixty years old. He added that the sons of Spaniards, born of white or Creole parents in the islands, were also unsuitable for training for the priesthood, since they had been reared by Filipina or by slave women, and consequently they had a very defective and uneducated upbringing. The only satisfactory solution, he averred, was to send from Spain exemplary priests who were zealous for the conversion of souls.[1] After several false starts, and in the face of much misgiving and unwillingness, a beginning was made with the formation of a Filipino native clergy at an unascertained date early in the eighteenth century. By 1754, at least four educational establishments in Manila were training native candidates for the priesthood. Some of the graduates had already been ordained, and were functioning as parish priests; but for the remainder of the colonial period, the Filipino secular clergy was still kept in strict subordination and inferiority to the Regular clergy of the religious Orders, just as the Indian clergy was in Goa down to the end of the eighteenth century. In the far-flung viceroyalties of Mexico and Peru, which between them covered virtually all of continental Spanish America during the seventeenth century, nothing was done to foster the development or even the foundation of a native Amerindian clergy. Control of the colonial Church through the *Patronato* was kept firmly in the hands of the peninsula-born higher clergy, although the Creole clergy steadily increased in importance and in number, and some of them even became bishops.

[1] Summary of Pardo's letter, Manila, 6 June 1680, in E. H. Blair and J. H. Robertson (eds.), *The Philippine Islands, 1493–1898* (55 vols., Cleveland, Ohio 1903–9), XLV, 182–3.

The problem of the native clergy

While the Portuguese and Spanish ecclesiastical and secular authorities were thus showing themselves to be either resolutely opposed to the formation of a native clergy in their respective colonial domains, or else determined to leave such a clergy in a strictly subordinate position, the attitude of the papacy was more forthcoming—at any rate in fits and starts. As early as 22 November 1630, the Sacred Congregation of the *Propaganda Fide* had promulgated with papal approval a decree which stated *inter alia* that the ordination of qualified Indian priests was highly desirable, and that one good Indian would reap more fruit than a hundred European priests. The papacy was also impressed by the need for a native clergy in countries which were not subject either in theory or in practice to the Spanish and Portuguese Crowns. In 1680, Pope Innocent XI told Mgr Pallu, Bishop of Heliopolis and Vicar-Apostolic of Tongking, on the eve of his departure for the Far East: 'We would rather learn that you have ordained one native priest than that you have baptized 50,000 pagans. The Jesuits have baptized many such, but subsequently their work has vanished in smoke because they did not ordain native priests.'[1] These were extreme views and hardly fair to the Jesuit missionaries labouring in Asia; although those working in China, for example, were for centuries divided among themselves as to how far a Chinese native clergy should be allowed to develop beyond a strictly subordinate role. But Pope Innocent XI's observation *does* reflect the increasing awareness at Rome that the formation of a native clergy was essential for the secure development of Christianity in Asia—if not in Latin America—and that the religious Orders were 'dragging their feet' in this respect, as indeed they were.

The first breach in the practice of white supremacy in the Church in Portuguese Asia came when some Goan secular priests were allowed to take the rule of the Oratory at the end of the seventeenth and beginning of the eighteenth century. It was these Goan priests, under the leadership of Fr Joseph Vaz, who

[1] R. Steele (trans.), *An Account of the State of the Roman Catholic Religion throughout the World, written for Pope Innocent XI by Monsignor Cerri* (London 1715), pp. 113–14.

not only saved the Roman Catholic Church in Ceylon from extinction at the hands of the Calvinist Dutch, but who set in motion a notable revival of its spiritual welfare. Yet despite the outstanding work done by these men in extremely dangerous and difficult circumstances, which cost some of them their lives, we find the Portuguese Archbishop of Goa in 1725 still vehemently denouncing the idea of a native or even of a *mestiço* clergy, and urging that only pure-born European whites should be employed in any responsible office. He held up as an example the colonial Church in Spanish America where, as he said, no Amerindians whatever were ordained, and only a very few and carefully selected *Mestizos*.[1]

It was that Jekyll-and-Hyde character the Marquis of Pombal, the virtual dictator of Portugal from 1755 to 1777, who did more to break down the ecclesiastical colour-bar than the papacy and the *Propaganda Fide* combined. His first move was the promulgation of the celebrated decree of 2 April 1761. This edict informed the viceroy of India and the governor-general of Moçambique that henceforth the East African and Asian subjects of the Portuguese Crown who were baptized Christians must be given exactly the same legal and social status as white persons who were born in Portugal, since 'His Majesty does not distinguish between his vassals by their colour but by their merits'. Moreover—and this was something new—it was made a criminal offence for white Portuguese to call their Indian fellow-subjects 'Niggers, *Mestiços*, dogs, bitches, and other insulting and opprobrious terms', as they were in the habit of doing.[2] This decree was repeated in even more categorical wording two years later; but the authorities at Goa showed themselves singularly reluctant to implement it, even though they knew that Pombal was not a man to be trifled with. More than ten years passed before anything was done, and then only because the Indian secular clergy of Goa sent a written protest to Pombal, complaining that the decrees of 1761–3 had never been implemented, and that they were still being kept in a strictly subordinate position by the archbishop. They alleged

[1] Fr Ignacio de Santa Tereza, 'Estado do prezente Estado da India' (original MS. Goa 1725, in the author's collection), fos. 49–51.
[2] J. H. Cunha Rivara (ed.), *Archivo Portuguez-Oriental*, VI (1876), 498–9.

that there were then over 10,000 native priests in Portuguese India—surely a great exaggeration—many of whom were fully qualified to fill vacant posts in the cathedral chapter and elsewhere. Yet the archbishop obstinately refused to appoint any of them, filling all vacancies with hurriedly ordained and semi-literate low-class Europeans, or even with 'illegitimate Chinese' from Macao.[1]

This representation produced a spirited reaction from Pombal. A new viceroy and a new archbishop were sent to Goa in 1774, with strict instructions not only to enforce the anti-colour-bar decrees which had been quietly shelved by their predecessors, but to favour the Indian secular clergy over and above the European Regular clergy, in cases where the claims of both to ecclesiastical preferment were roughly equal. Pombal reminded the new archbishop that by canon law the Regular clergy could only act as parish priests in mission territory, or in emergencies when no suitable secular clergy were available. Portuguese India was no longer mission territory, nor had it been for many years. The indigenous clergy now contained many more exemplary and learned priests than did the mendicant Orders, which were in an advanced state of decay.[2]

The gentle pressure exercised from Rome by the *Propaganda Fide*, the more forceful pressure applied by Pombal, together with the great and growing scarcity of missionary vocations from Europe after the suppression of the Jesuits (in the Portuguese empire) in 1760—all these factors combined to improve the relative position of the Indian clergy during the last half of the eighteenth century. The Theatines at Goa had led the way by admitting Indian vocations in 1750, and the older mendicant Orders gradually followed this lead. By the time of their suppression throughout Portuguese territory in 1835, out of some 300 regular clergy in Goa, only sixteen were Europeans, all the others being sons of the soil.[3]

---

[1] Petition of the indigenous secular clergy of Goa in C. Lagrange Monteiro de Barbuda (ed.), *Instrucções com que El-Rei D. José I mandou passar ao Estado da India o Governador e Capitão General, e o Arcebispo Primaz do Oriente no anno de 1774* (Pangim 1841), II, 13–14.

[2] *Instrucções...ao Estado da India...no anno de 1774* (ed. 1841), *passim*.

[3] C. Merces de Melo, S.J., *Native Clergy in India*, pp. 172–4.

But although Pombal's egalitarian policy in this respect was continued after his fall by the home government under Queen D. Maria I, the prelates of Portuguese India were still reluctant to promote Indian priests to high ecclesiastical office at Goa. This in turn fanned the frustration and discontent—not to say the ambitions—of the disgruntled indigenous clergy, whose dissatisfaction culminated in the 'conspiracy of the Pintos' in 1787. This conspiracy was an abortive plot, which had as its objective the expulsion of the Portuguese and the formation of a self-governing republic at Goa. Out of forty-seven plotters arrested by the Portuguese authorities, the seventeen ringleaders were Indian priests. Their cloth saved them from the fate of fifteen of their fellow-plotters who were executed in circumstances of great barbarity; but the priests were sent to Lisbon, ostensibly for trial. They were never brought before any legal court but were deliberately left to rot in prison, where several of them died. The survivors were amnestied in 1807, when they were too old and ill to be a danger to anybody.[1] Not until 1835 did a Goan priest become administrator of the vacant archbishopric for two years, and not until a few years ago did a priest of Goan origin become a cardinal.

Here again there is a close parallel with developments in the Spanish colonial empire and in Brazil, where the religious Orders systematically prevented (in so far as they could) the development of anything more than a second-rate secular clergy whom they kept in a strictly subordinate position. As in Portuguese India, so in Spanish America, Brazil, and the Philippines, an antagonism developed between the European-born clergy and the indigenous or *Mestizo* clergy, which degenerated into national and racial enmity. In both the Iberian colonial empires, this contempt of the white man for the brown was often extended to the Creole clergy born of white or near-white parents. These men were likewise usually excluded from high ecclesiastical office and kept in a subordinate position to the peninsula-born. Hence among the protagonists of the Independence movements in Mexico and Brazil, as well as in Goa and in the Philippines, we find the native

[1] J. H. Cunha Rivara, *A Conjuração de 1787 em Goa* (Nova Goa 1875).

and *mestizo* secular clergy strongly represented in the early nineteenth century.[1] As Fr Horacio de la Costa, the first Filipino Jesuit to be appointed Provincial of the Society in his native land, has observed in his essay on this problem: 'It is always bad statesmanship, in the long run, to put political expediency before the demands of the spiritual order'.[2] In other words, if I may, as the Portuguese proverb says, 'ensinar o Padre Nosso ao vigario' ('teach the vicar the Lord's Prayer'), 'whatsoever a man soweth, that shall he also reap' (Galatians, vi. 7).

[1] Hidalgo in Mexico; the ecclesiastics involved in the embryo Independence movements of Minas Gerais (1789) and Goa (1787), and the Filipino priests unfrocked and executed at Cavite (1872), are a few of the many instances that come to mind.

[2] H. de la Costa, S.J., 'Development of the native clergy in the Philippines', p. 247.

A CHRISTIAN EXPERIMENT: THE EARLY SIERRA LEONE COLONY

by A. F. WALLS

IN the course of the past century the centre of gravity of the Christian world has shifted completely. Europe, once the centre, is now at best an outpost on the fringe of the Christian world, some would say an outpost likely to be overwhelmed. The great majority of Christians, and the overwhelming majority of practising Christians are, and are clearly going to be, Africans, Americans or Asians. And of these, the most startling expansion—the greatest Christian expansion since what were for Europe the Middle Ages—has been in Africa, where Christians have been increasing in geometrical progression, doubling their numbers every twelve years or so, for over a century. The greater part of African Church history, however, has still to be written. Hagiography we have in abundance, and hagiography, like mythology, is a valid literary genre; but (again like mythology) it is a poetic, not a scholarly category. Of missionary history we have a little, though very little in proportion to the vast resources which the missionary society archives supply; but missionary history is only one specialized part of African Church history; by far the greater part of African Christian life and African Christian expansion goes on, and has long gone on, without the presence, let alone the superintendence, of the European missionary.

The first modern Church of tropical Africa with a continuous history to the present day is that of the Sierra Leone colony.[1] The colony was itself a sort of stepchild of the Evangelical Revival, and

---

[1] This description is intended to distinguish it from those churches which derive directly from the ancient churches of Egypt and Ethiopia, or from Counter-Reformation missionary activity; and from the chaplaincies to European residents, which sometimes touched some Africans, in the forts and factories of Britain, Holland, Denmark and Brandenburg.

in its early days reflects the two ways in which the Evangelicals were to alter British attitudes to Africa: by institutionalizing and making respectable (and in a measure effective) opposition to the slave trade, and in the growth of the overseas missionary movement. In the creation of the Sierra Leone colony the humanitarian and missionary concerns of Clapham Evangelicalism, together with their economic theory and commercial interests, met together. This 'Province of Freedom'—the phrase is Granville Sharp's[1]—on the west coast of Africa was to be a haven from the slave trade. Its orderly, industrious, and virtuous society was to be a pattern to the continent. Its prosperity—it was assumed that it would be prosperous—was to be the continent's envy, causing chiefs and peoples to abandon the slave trade as less profitable than an export trade in raw materials and agricultural produce. And its Christian character was to facilitate the evangelization of Africa, both by creating a Christian presence and by serving as a springboard for missionaries to the interior.

The first attempt to realize these visions, by means of a party of destitute Negroes and Lascars from the British cities, leavened, probably accidentally, by London prostitutes, was an almost unmitigated failure.[2] The real founding fathers of the Sierra Leone colony were 1,100 men and women, Africans or of African descent, who arrived from Nova Scotia in 1792, and marched from the shore singing 'Awake and sing the song of Moses and the Lamb'.[3] Most of them had been slaves in North America; many, indeed, had been born in slavery. Now they were entering their promised land, and celebrated the crossing of the Red Sea with an appropriate song of Miriam. We may note in passing that the modern Church of tropical Africa did not begin by missionary agency at all; it arrived, a ready-made African Church.

The Nova Scotian settlers of 1792 were children of the Evangelical Revival. Many knew of evangelical experience and spoke

[1] C. B. Wadstrom, *An Essay on Colonization* (London 1794), p. 338.
[2] On the Sierra Leone colony as a whole see the admirable *History of Sierra Leone* by Christopher Fyfe (Oxford 1962). Cf. R. R. Kuczynski, *Demographic Survey of the British Colonial Empire*, 1 (London 1948).
[3] J. B. Elliott, *Lady Huntingdon's Connexion in Sierra Leone: a Narrative of its History and Present State* (London 1851), p. 14.

evangelical language as intimately as the Clapham philanthropists who planned and financed the settlement; though it was a more boisterous phase of evangelical religion that most of them represented.[1] It is clear that they came as Christians, bringing their own churches, preachers, and church organization and discipline with them; and all visitors to Freetown seem to have been struck by their religious activity. The Directors of the Company reported in 1795:

On that day [Sunday] they abstain entirely from work, dress themselves in very good (and some even in very gay) attire, and repair together with their children to church, where their whole deportment during the service, and their whole appearance are represented to be such as form a very striking spectacle...

The Nova Scotians are not only punctual at their worship, but many of them profess also in other respects much regard to religion. It is natural however to imagine that among such a body of men, almost all of them claiming to be thought Christians, there will be some who have imbibed very inadequate or enthusiastic notions of Christianity; a few perhaps who set up hypocritical pretensions to it; while there may be many others who, notwithstanding some defects in their religious knowledge, may be consistent and sincere Christians. There are five or six black preachers among them, raised up from their own body, who are not without a considerable influence; and it is supposed that the discipline which they preserve in their little congregations has contributed materially to the maintenance of the general morals which have been spoken of.[2]

A visiting sea-captain notes in his log: 'They appear very Religious attending Service by 3 o'clock in the Morning and till Eleven at night, four, or five, times per week...'[3] And an English lady, usually rather tart in her references to religion, remarked: 'I never met with, heard, or read of, any set of people observing the same appearance of godliness; for I do not remember, since they first landed here, my ever awaking (and I have awoke at every hour of

---

[1] Cf. A. F. Walls, 'The Nova Scotian settlers and their religion', *Sierra Leone Bulletin of Religion*, 1 (1959), 19–31.

[2] *An Account of the Colony of Sierra Leone*, 2nd ed. (1795), p. 80.

[3] Samuel Gamble, captain of the *Sandown*; see A. P. Kup, 'Freetown in 1794', *Sierra Leone Studies*, n.s., XI (1958), 163.

the night), without hearing preachings from some quarter or other.'[1]

Thus did Sierra Leone appear indeed to be, in Wilberforce's phrase, the Morning Star of Africa. With a sober, prosperous, worshipping Christian community settled on the west coast of Africa, surely the time was at hand when Ethiopia should stretch out her hands unto God.

A very few years brought disillusion and frustration. The settlers who had expected a land flowing with milk and honey, and in whose government they would share as the elders of Israel, found in that green but barren land no milk, no honey, and not as much land as they expected; found government alien and grasping; and the Christian commonwealth, while it continued to sing and pray, became a community with a settled grievance and increasing mistrust of Europeans, however generous their professions. Besides the traumatic experience of slavery to European masters, they now felt they had three times been tricked and betrayed by Authority, each time a European authority. They had originally enlisted in the British army in the American War of Independence, on the promise of liberty and lands when the war ended. The promise of land had, of course, been made on the assumption of British victory; and the victory of the American rebels gave the British government the embarrassing problem of how to dispose of their loyal soldiers. Nova Scotia—at this time still a land with much virgin forest—was the expedient adopted, but in Nova Scotia there were also white loyalists, people who had given up estates in the revolted colonies in loyalty to the Crown. The black ex-soldiers waited and shivered, but lands were desperately slow in coming; and, they complained, it was whites that were served first. When the proposal came of land of their own in Sierra Leone many leaped at the chance. Too many; the Sierra Leone Company had the embarrassment of having promised, through its agents, more than it could fulfil. With the introduction of a quit rent (regarded by the administration as a property tax, for overheads, but by the settlers as a deprivation of title) the breach became a gulf. Europeans, however fair their speech and loud their Christian pro-

[1] Anna Maria Falconbridge, *Two Voyages to Sierra Leone* (London 1794), p. 201.

fession, were untrustworthy, sharp practisers and, above all, always out to deny the black men land.[1] Part of the settlement erupted in armed rebellion in 1800, and to add insult to injury, the rebellion was put down with the help of the pagan Maroons, newly arrived in the colony.

Nor were the Clapham philanthropists any better pleased. They had expected the settlers to be grateful and dutiful for all that had been done; instead, they were disgruntled and rebellious. Again, the economic theory on which the colony had been based was simply not working out in practice. Far from making a profit, the Directors had steadily to record a loss. Each year's report informed shareholders with regret of the exceptional circumstances which had prevented a profit in the past year, and of the hopes for profit in the following year. Meanwhile the pro-slavery lobby was using the failure and discontent to pour ridicule on the whole cause of abolition.

Nor was there much to show for the other bright hope of Sierra Leone, its being the beacon light to Africa, the springboard of missionary enterprise. The Sierra Leone peninsula, a strip of which had been acquired for the original settlement, and its neighbourhood were not thickly populated. From the first, sporadic attempts were made by Nova Scotians and Company government alike, to evangelize these peoples; but, under the pressing weight of the colony's own affairs, none of these was followed up with much drive. In the Sierra Leone river lay slave factories—neighbours of the colony with which, however distasteful it might be, the colony had to have neighbourly relations. The factories depended on supplies of slaves from the lands beyond, and it was to these lands of the middlemen that much of the early missionary effort was directed. The area was partly, but not entirely, Islamized; and behind lay Muslim lands, ruled by the Fula builders of the empire in the Futa Jallon. With some of the nearer of these the colony had made contact. Islam and its book perhaps seemed less alien and more comprehensible than African traditional religion;

[1] R. W. July, *The Origins of Modern Africa Thought* (London 1968), pp. 48–66; P. E. H. Hair, Christianity at Freetown from 1792 as a field for research, *Urbanisation in African Social Change* (Edinburgh 1963), pp. 127–40.

and Timbuktu, though centuries past its prime, still had a fascination for the Western mind, which thought of it still as the centre of a golden Islamic civilization. At any rate, missionary strategists of the period talk with obvious enthusiasm of anything which promises access to the Muslim heartlands of the West African savannahs, which have, as things have turned out, never been responsive to Christian preaching. For the early phase of the modern missionary movement, the Sierra Leone hinterland became a sort of rusk on which infant missionary societies cut their teeth. It need hardly be added that rusks are seldom anyone's favourite diet once the teeth are through.

It is not a very inspiring story.[1] The Baptists sent two men. One was young and feeble, and had to be sent home quickly; the other got heavily involved in Freetown politics, and was extradited. The Methodists sent a whole party of local preachers as an agricultural mission to the Fula at Timbo; but, to the great relief of everyone who saw them in Freetown, they never got beyond the colony's borders. One of them began unpromisingly by shaking his fist in the face of the first Muslim he met and telling him Muhammad was a false prophet; and the wives, when they realized that it was a country where it would be difficult to do any regular shopping, decided to return to the ship, taking their husbands with them.[2] Of the agents of the London and Glasgow Missionary Societies who survived beyond the first few months, one proved unsatisfactory physically and one morally; one left to become a lecturer in the cause of atheism[3] and one to be a slave-dealer. The Edinburgh Missionary Society, after a shaky start (their two Presbyterians, with two Glasgow men, travelled on the same boat as the London Society's Independents, and by the time they reached Freetown the whole ship had been devastated by an outbreak of *rabies theologorum*), did rather better; but within a few

[1] The outlines are in C. P. Groves, *The Planting of Christianity in Africa* (London 1948), I, 208 ff.

[2] Zachary Macaulay's mordant account is in his journals, in the Huntingdon Library, California. A version appears in Viscountess Knutsford, *Life and Letters of Zachary Macaulay* (London 1901), pp. 116 ff.

[3] William Brown, *History of the Propagation of Christianity* (Edinburgh 1854), II, 450.

years one had been murdered for his possessions and the other, Henry Brunton of Selkirk, left Africa to spend the remainder of his missionary service among the Tartar tribes of the Russian Empire.

Brunton's work was inherited by the Church Missionary Society which, though founded in 1799, could not, because of the principles on which it recruited, get its missionaries on to the field until 1804, when it sent the first of a series of German Lutheran candidates to Sierra Leone to reopen Christian enterprise in the area known as the Rio Pongas, to the Susu, a people then less markedly Muslim than now.

The CMS provided the most considerable of the early missions which attempted to use Sierra Leone as a base for the interior.[1] The principal way of approach was by means of a school. The theory behind this seems to have been first, that very little could be done with adults; and second, that it should be easier to wean children away from pagan influences.[2] In any case, despite the grammar Brunton had prepared, the missionaries did not have enough Susu to preach in it. We have, therefore, the incongruous spectacle of a school for Susu children taught entirely in English, entirely by Germans. One or two of the boys did well; at least one came to England, piously lived, and soon succumbing to the climate, serenely died, and became the subject of an edifying tract;[3] but what was the prospect of the boys continuing to do well once they returned to take their place in the pagan or Muslim family and village? Others turned out less well, and the mission suffered from incendiarism. For twenty years the Sierra Leone colony had been used as the base for missionary operations in the interior. No less than six missionary societies had initiated operations there. Not one could be counted even a moderate success, and only one was being continued by the mission which started it.

Meanwhile, both the government and population of the colony

---

[1] E. Stock, *History of the Church Missionary Society* (London 1899), I, 82 ff.
[2] CMS Archives, CAI | E 5.
[3] E. Bickersteth, *A Memoir of Simeon Wilhelm, a Native of the Susoo Country in West Africa* (London 1818(?), 6th ed. 1839).

were being transformed. Close on the passing of the act of 1807 which made the slave trade an illegal occupation for British citizens, Sierra Leone passed from the hands of the Sierra Leone Company to those of the British government, and the British Navy acquired the use of one of the two most magnificent natural harbours in Africa, enabling a naval squadron to be stationed in a position to intercept vessels carrying slaves. Though the British government for some years tended to consult the men of Clapham on matters relating to Sierra Leone, the province of freedom was no longer the responsibility of private Christian philanthropy. From 1808 it was a colony of the Crown.

The population likewise was diversified from several different sources. First, as we have mentioned, came the Maroons, formerly slaves in Jamaica, defeated heroes of a fierce guerrilla war and, like the settlers of 1792, unsuccessfully grafted into Nova Scotia. In Nova Scotia they had acquiesced in lectures on Christianity but their Christian veneer was of the thinnest.[1] There were disbanded soldiers and even convicts from the West Indies; above all, after 1808 there were the cargoes of the intercepted slave ships, brought into Freetown from every part of West Africa from Senegal to the Congo; at first a trickle, then a flood, till Nova Scotians and Maroons alike were overshadowed by the new population which had never known life across the Atlantic.

The Christianity of early Freetown deserves rather closer attention, particularly in its relations with European missionaries. As we have seen the colony's oldest churches were not of missionary origin: congregations of Baptists, Methodists, and the Countess of Huntingdon's Connexion were present and active from the first day of the colony's establishment.[2] It was nearly twenty years

---

[1] R. C. Dallas, *History of the Maroons* (London 1803), II, 221 ff.

[2] Elliott, *Lady Huntingdon's Connexion in Sierra Leone*; Thomas Coke, *An Interesting Narrative of a Mission sent to Sierra Leone*...(London 1812). Melvill Horne, chaplain to the Company, estimated that 300 out of the 750 adults were 'under a religious profession' (i.e. what Coke calls 'serious characters'), two-thirds of them Methodists, the other third divided between the Baptists and Huntingdonians (letter to Thomas Haweis in the possession of Mr Christopher Fyfe). On David George, the much-respected Baptist pastor, see A. H. M. Kirk-Greene, 'David George: the Nova Scotian experience', *Sierra Leone Studies* n.s., XIV (1960), 93–120.

after that before the first Methodist missionary arrived; and the Methodists were alone in Freetown having close relations with their colleagues in Britain.

The origins of Freetown Methodism lie then in Nova Scotia. The minutes of the Methodist Conference of 1790 give the number in society in Nova Scotia as 800, of whom a quarter are described as 'blacks'. The colony was, to use the modern jargon, in a state of rapid social change. To the sparse colony-born population of principally English and Scottish origin—often liberal, even republican, in sentiment, and no great lovers of the Church of England—were added the white loyalists from the South, very self-consciously British and staunchly Anglican, as well as the Negroes. As the latter received or renewed the impress of Evangelical religion from the colony's fervent preachers they saw the Church of England, as represented in the local chaplains appointed through the Society for the Propagation of the Gospel, unsympathetic or hostile to the preaching and experience they knew; they would see it also as the church of the White Loyalists, the people whom government favoured at their expense, the people who got grants of land while promises to Negroes remained unfulfilled. They would see also the Church of England becoming in effect the State Church of the colony, though representing only a minority of its population. Unlike most British Methodists, the Methodists of Nova Scotia, black or white, knew a Methodism which had never really been inside the Church of England. It is worth noting that when some time afterwards Conference came to send out a superintendent from Britain to Nova Scotia he was a disastrous failure because he tried to impose a British pattern completely alien to the Nova Scotian experience.[1]

These things may help to explain the touchiness and readiness to take offence which the Nova Scotian community seems so often to have demonstrated, and it is evident from the journal of Zachary Macaulay, first Councillor and then Governor of the colony, that

[1] M. W. Armstrong, *The Great Awakening in Nova Scotia, 1776–1809* (Hartford, Conn. 1948); W. C. Barclay, *Early American Methodism*, 1 (New York 1949); G. G. Findlay and W.W. Holdsworth, *History of the Wesleyan Missionary Society*, 1 (London 1921).

some of the strongest opposition to the Company's government in the period before 1800 was centred in the Methodist society. To an extreme sensitivity on matters political was added a hardly veiled hostility to what the settlers called the 'established Church', that is, the colonial chaplaincy. Now the Company had guaranteed, and conscientiously observed, complete freedom of religion. The various congregations saw to their own affairs, and no one ever thought of the chaplaincy as superseding, or ever doing more than supplementing them; nor were the chaplains always Anglican. The first two, Nathaniel Gilbert and Melvill Horne, though both in Anglican orders, had unimpeachable Methodist backgrounds and connections. But though Horne had itinerated with Wesley, he was a complete failure with the Freetown Methodists. His official position identified him with the Company's government at a time when that government was becoming extremely unpopular; and it is probable that at no time could many of them have recognized in that rather scatterbrained English clergyman the Methodism they knew in Nova Scotia.

The years of frustration and bitterness took their toll. When the first Methodist missionary arrived in 1811, he found 110 members in society, about half the number on the books in 1792, though the population of the colony had quadrupled in the interim.[1] A certain fragmentation had also occurred, and we hear of various splinter churches.[2]

Nevertheless, the Freetown Methodists of this period and through the succeeding years began to exercise an influence on many of the essentially pagan Maroons, despite the fact that relations between settlers and Maroons as a whole were frequently bad and sometimes violent. The Maroon community, docile from the time of its landing as far as government was concerned, gradually assimilated to the established ways of the colony; and in most of those ways, including religion, the Nova Scotian settlers set the tone. Certainly well before the arrival of the first missionaries, Freetown Methodists had seen the conversion of the Maroons as

[1] George Warren in *Methodist Magazine*, xxv (n.s., IX) (1812), 317. The originals of Warren's two letters in the *Methodist Magazine* appear to be missing.
[2] Ibid.; cf. Coke, *An Interesting Narrative*, pp. 24 ff.

part of their responsibility, and Maroons of the younger generation were attending society.[1]

This society preserved both the framework of Methodist organization and the principal elements of Methodist discipline. Both the early missionaries, George Warren in 1811 and William Davies in 1815, reported with surprise that this was so,[2] and Zachary Macaulay, who possessed a built-in resistance to most forms of human blandishment, confessed himself deeply impressed with the spirituality of a man like Joseph Brown, the senior local preacher.[3] The Wesleyan missionaries also found religious experience and a vocabulary describing it which they understood: 'mourning for sin'—that is, the conviction of personal guilt; 'enjoying the divine favour'—that is, possessing the sense of personal forgiveness, which might come soon or late after this conviction; 'groaning for full redemption', 'seeking liberty', that is, looking for complete freedom from inbred sin. For example, Davies mentions one Prince Edward, who had been wild and trifling, but was convicted under one of Davies's earliest sermons. He thereafter attended both service and class meeting regularly, but always in evident gloom or distress. Then one day he confessed to Davies that he could not expect pardon from God unless he married the woman he was living with. This at length he did, and also made her, protesting, attend Mrs Davies's class meeting. Within a week she was 'groaning for deliverance'; and a week later still appeared at the class meeting very cheerful, 'with a clear testimony of acceptance with God and enjoyment of pardoning love'. But her unfortunate husband, convinced of sin so long before, remained just where he was.

It was three months later, according to Davies's journal, that

---

[1] Cf. C. Marke, *Origins of Wesleyan Methodism in Sierra Leone* (London 1913), pp. 12 f. That receptives were also in view is shown, e.g. by *Methodist Magazine*, XXV (n.s., IX) (1812), 639 (settler leaders introduce Warren to interested receptives) and MMS Archives, James Wise and others to Wood, April 1816.

[2] Warren, *Methodist Magazine*, XXV (n.s., IX) (1812), 637–9; W. Davies to Buckley, MMS Archives, 20 February 1815 (all references to MMS Archives are to Sierra Leone Box 1).

[3] Macaulay, journals (above, p. 112 n. 2): 'One of the most humble Christians I have ever met with'.

Prince Edward burst in while Davies was kneeling in prayer and picked him up in his arms shouting 'I found him, I found him!'

I asked what he had found. 'I found Christ. I feel his pardoning presence. His spirit says, Go in peace, all thy sins are forgiven thee.'[1]

This story, of course, could be paralleled in every detail of language a hundred times over in English or North American Methodism; and at least one celebrated preacher in England was capable of cavorting with a converted vicar in his arms.[2]

The insistence of classical Methodism on preparedness for death is paralleled in this story, related by Davies in a letter to the missionary society:

[A certain young woman—a member of class, but without the assurance of salvation—had died.]
About three nights before she died she was seeking the Lord continually ...Upon [her] deathbed the Lord manifested himself. She called her grandmother (who is also a Methodist) in the night to tell her what God had done for her soul. Said she 'Praise the Lord he hath pardoned my sins his sweet voice said to my soul, Arise shine thy light is come and the glory of the Lord is written upon thy heart go in peace and sin no more. I must see my class Mistress to tell her also what God hath done for my soul.' In the morning Mrs Davies went to see her and found her in great pain, yet enjoying the liberty of God's children. About half an hour before she died, she had a hard struggle with the enemy. She said I have just escaped Hell, Satan would have me in, but the Lord delivered me and when I escaped another soul dropt in.[3]

Not surprisingly, the last quaint touch was crossed out in London when the letter was prepared for publication.

Nor need we think of the Freetown society as aping what they did not understand. We have already seen that neither missionary had any serious fault to find with discipline or organization.

Warren recorded his impressions of a sermon preached soon after his arrival by the veteran blind preacher, Moses Wilkinson:

[1] *Extracts from the Journal of the Rev. William Davies, 1st, when a missionary at Sierra Leone, Western Africa* (Llanidloes 1835), *s.v.* September 1815, 4 February 1816.
[2] Cf. F. W. Bourne, *The King's Son: a Memoir of Billy Bray* (London 1871, many editions).
[3] MMS Archives, Davies to Buckley, 10 August 1815.

Moses Wilkinson preached this evening, from Isaiah iii, 11 and 12. He gave out his hymns and text from memory. His manner was warm and animating. He seemed to strive at keeping close to his text, and made, in the course of his sermon, several useful observations. While hearing him I was led to admire the goodness and wisdom of God in the instruments which he frequently sees fit to use, to advance the interests of his kingdom. Many of the wise and learned in this world, if they were to see and hear such a man as our brother, professedly engaging in endeavouring to lead their fellow creatures from sin to holiness, would at once conclude it to be impossible for them to effect the object which they have in view. Experience, however, flatly contradicts such a conclusion. Numbers have been led by their means to change their lives, and are induced from day to day to pursue that conduct which conduces to their own happiness and to the welfare of those that are around them.[1]

With this in mind we may consider the society's relationship to the missionaries; and at once we are aware of a strange ambivalence. On the one hand, there was in the settler population, as we have seen, a deep-seated resentment at and suspicion of Europeans; on the other, the settler society was very self-consciously Methodist, proudly if somewhat intermittently maintaining its contacts with the Methodist Conference. It addressed a number of appeals to Conference to send a preacher. One which attracted particular attention, written by Joseph Brown, appeared in the *Methodist Magazine* in 1807; Conference (or Dr Coke) politely answered the various appeals, but it was not until 1811 that the preacher requested was actually sent.[2] George Warren, who arrived that year, had the warmest possible reception—though the society politely insisted on seeing his letter from Conference. Moses Wilkinson, now very old, blind and lame, averred that 'about two months since, it was strongly impressed upon his mind that a person was coming to take charge of them, and that he was already on his way'.[3] The leader of a splinter society offered to rejoin the

---

[1] *Methodist Magazine*, xxv (n.s., ix) (1812), 637–9.
[2] Brown's letter, dated 5 July 1806, indicates that he had made a similar request two years earlier but had received no answer. Coke, *An Interesting Narrative*, pp. 17 ff., says 'many' letters were received on this topic over the years.
[3] Coke, *An Interesting Narrative*, pp. 24 ff.

main body and bring his flock with him. In the first few months of Warren's ministry the congregation and the society increased, and it was noted particularly that backsliders were returning.[1]

On his first Sunday there was one signal from the society of what they expected of their missionary. They inquired particularly if he were legally qualified to administer the sacrament. On learning that he was, there was an outburst of joy, and a clear indication that the society wished for the sacrament in their own chapel.[2]

In the early days of the Sierra Leone colony the Company chaplain had administered the sacrament—in fact, Methodists were sometimes apt to assert that this was his only function.[3] Long since, the society and the chaplaincy had gone their separate ways; but, in accordance with old custom and official Methodist discipline, members continued to attend the communion service in the chaplaincy. For the sacrament to be regularly administered in the Methodist chapel at the hands of an English minister with the full authority of Conference, would be the final and most effective repudiation of contact between the society and the established church of the government. Warren was very willing to accede; though caution and a care for relations with the chaplain led him, like many of his brethren in England under similar pressures, to stipulate that no administration should occur when there was a communion service at 'the church', and that those who wished to receive communion at the chaplaincy were at liberty to do so.[4] A major point, however, had been gained by the society: the arrival of their missionary had sharpened their identity and their distinction from the church of the government. They now lacked nothing.

But within eight months, Warren was dead. More than three years elapsed before his successor appeared in Sierra Leone: an ardent young Welshman called William Davies with his wife Jane. He was welcomed by the Freetown Methodists with the cordiality they had extended to Warren, and large congregations

[1] Ibid. pp. 30 ff.
[2] *Methodist Magazine*, xxv (n.s., ix) (1812), 638 f.
[3] Cf. Knutsford, *Life...of Zachary Macaulay*, pp. 136 ff.
[4] *Methodist Magazine*, xxv (n.s., ix) (1812), 638 f.

came to hear him preach and 'read the prayers of the Church of England'.[1] He in his turn was deeply impressed as he talked to the leaders of the society. All the signs of spiritual awakening seemed present: the preaching, the prayer meetings, the class meetings, all seemed to evidence it, and Davies writes cheerfully 'A prospect of seeing good days in this place'.[2]

But clouds fell across these good days. First came the question of a school, which brought to the surface differing conceptions on the part of the missionary and the Methodist settler community. With Warren had come out three schoolmasters, and a school had been established in connection with the chapel. The main expense of this was on the mission. Davies declared that the school was not touching the neediest class, the recaptives, but only the children of settlers and Maroons, many of whom were in a better position to pay than the Welsh poor. Accordingly he closed it, and opened a boys' school under his own direction and a girls' school under that of his wife. He administered these schools, not on behalf of the mission, but on behalf of the government. Governor Mac-Carthy applauded the fact that he undertook this duty without fee or reward; but the action would not commend itself in every part of the community.[3] Here was the missionary removing one of the props of settler Methodism, one of its distinctive institutions, initiated by agents fof the Methodist Conference, supported by funds from England, and instead undertaking service on behalf of a government for which the settlers felt little sympathy.

A second, and recurrent, source of tension was finance, which had never really been set in order since the beginning of the mission.[4] English Methodism had been used to the preachers being supported by the circuits, and it had been assumed that a similar pattern would develop in Sierra Leone. It did not so develop. The society had been regulating its own affairs for years

[1] MMS Archives, Davies to Buckley, 20 February 1815.
[2] *Journal*, *s.v.* 26 February 1815.
[3] *Journal*, Introduction; cf. letter from Sir C. MacCarthy, printed as appendix; and MMS Archives, Davies to Buckley, 19 December 1815. The schools' daily orders are in MMS Archives, Sierra Leone Box 1.
[4] Cf. MMS Archives, Hirst and Healey to Coke, 21 April 1812 (*sic*, though clearly a slip for 1813), and 16 June 1813; the same to Blanshard, 20 July 1814.

before the missionaries came; it welcomed the missionaries as assistance and recognition from the Conference which had been regarded by the settlers with reverence from Nova Scotian days. The arrival of missionaries and the institutions taken in hand by them vastly increased Methodist expenditure, for the cost of living in European fashion was extremely high; but it is very doubtful if the Freetown society ever seriously expected to be given responsibility for any considerable part of this new expenditure. Was it not the work of Conference, which naturally wanted to assist a small outpost of Methodism? Why should a missionary of the Conference be on a different basis from the stipendiary missionaries of the Church Missionary Society, who even got an allowance of cloth? This point is forcefully made in a letter in the name of the Freetown society leaders, apparently drafted by James Wise, the government printer, which reflects a literary competence equal to that of any of the early missionaries.[1] The fathers and brethren in London who received such letters, however, could only wonder at the large bills which continued to be sent in by the mission, and hope that the good Methodist principle of circuit support would at last, and before too long, be established in Freetown. Davies, caught between two firm-minded bodies, neither of whom saw any reason why they should substantially increase their contributions, effected a compromise; more and more he came to support himself on government emoluments.

This brings us to the greatest stumbling block of all, and one in which the attitudes and reflexes of official British Methodism were quite different from those of the Methodism of Nova Scotia or Freetown. British Methodism had been highly sensitive to any suggestion that it was a subversive movement, and very concerned to profess its essential loyalty, that the command to 'Honour the king' followed very naturally upon that to 'Fear God'. Sidmouth's bill of 1811 which demanded, *inter alia*, of each applicant for a preaching licence the recommendation of six 'substantial and reputable' householders in his own congregation, was partly inspired by the growing strength of Methodism, and partly conditioned by the belief that this growing strength was subversive of public

[1] MMS Archives, James Wise and others to Wood, April 1816.

order. The measure was killed, but the need to assert Methodist loyalty was increased by it. The affair of the Sidmouth Bill also put Methodists into a position which they disliked and sought to avoid: of being classed as dissenters, and having, like other dissenters, to be watchful of their privileges and status in law. This was uncongenial to those who, as the Conference of 1812 said in its address to the societies 'considered themselves as belonging to the Church of England'—whether or not Conference was justified in adding 'of which class the great bulk of our Societies is composed'.[1] Methodists of this stamp were quite unlike the older dissenting bodies, such as the Baptists and Independents, in whom a long tradition of disabilities inflicted by Church and State had produced a not unnatural tendency to political radicalism and republicanism, and a very sharp anti-Anglican feeling.

These features of the dissenting tradition were, however, as we have seen, established features of the life of Freetown Methodists. They were shared also by many Methodists in Nova Scotia, and also by one European who seems to have got on well with the Freetown Methodists, a Company schoolmaster called Garvin, back in Macaulay's time.[2] Probably to the Freetown society Garvin looked more like a 'real Methodist' than any European they had met since Nova Scotian days.

William Davies, however, was no Garvin; he was very much a standard-product Wesleyan minister of his own day, simplistic in his loyalty to the king and with no bitterness against the Church of England. While the leaders of Freetown Methodism were talking of the sloth and avarice of the 'carnal Merchant missionaries' of the CMS and even of their 'Church (so-called)',[3] Davies was establishing most cordial relations with the CMS missionary who was now colonial chaplain, Leopold Butscher. Butscher used to attend the Methodist chapel on Sunday evenings, sitting up in the pulpit behind Davies, and giving an additional sermon if, as Davies put it, 'he thinks that I have not preached long enough, or well enough'. And as for the communion service, which at one

[1] Cf. A. W. Harrison, *The separation of Methodism from the Church of England* (London 1945), pp. 29 ff.
[2] Fyfe, *History of Sierra Leone*, pp. 69 f., 650.
[3] Wise and others to Wood, MMS Archives, April 1816.

time seemed to be the symbol of the Methodists' self-sufficiency, not only did Butscher share in the administration twice a quarter; once a quarter, Davies assisted him in the church, there was no morning service in the chapel, and the society once more attended service in the 'established church'.[1]

From one point of view, these developments were a pleasing expression of Christian unity; from another, they were imposing dangerous strains on unity. The hardness of attitudes must not be exaggerated; and after all, Butscher was no High Church parson, but a German Lutheran whose wife was actually an English Methodist. There was always contact and fellowship between the Christian communities in Freetown, and the united missionary prayer meeting, in which Butscher joined, was held not only in the Methodist chapel but in the Baptist and Huntingdonian churches, which had no European oversight.[2] But, given the history and suspicions of the Nova Scotian Methodists, anything which looked like an alliance of Europeans, Government, and the established Church was potentially explosive, and that the Governor smiled upon the development of ecumenicity would do it but little service among them.

Governor MacCarthy smiled on Davies and all his works. Entirely dedicated to the ideal of a unified Christian civilization in Sierra Leone, to which the increasing numbers of recaptives would be assimilated, he found in Davies a very useful agent. That this co-operative European, a man with sensible ideas about the education of the recaptives and energy in attending to it, should have official charge of the Methodist society, hitherto one of the centres of Nova Scotian fractiousness, must have seemed great good fortune. He made Davies an alderman of Freetown;[3] later he was to make him mayor. Davies says MacCarthy was 'like a father to me in all things'.[4] Edward Bickersteth, visiting the CMS mission on behalf of the parent committee, was welcomed by Davies, whom he describes as having always shown himself friendly to the established Church.[5] The credit of the Methodist society in the eyes

[1] Davies, *Journal*, p. 37.
[2] Ibid. The building used for the chaplaincy had no lights, which made it unsuitable for evening use.   [3] Davies, *Journal*, s.v. 7 February 1816.
[4] Ibid. p. 53.   [5] CMS Archives, CAI | E 5.

of the small but influential body of Europeans began to rise: 'European gentlemen of all persuasions' subscribed to the new Methodist chapel.[1] The time was not far distant when they wanted their subscriptions back.[2]

For relations between Davies and the society steadily deteriorated. How far his own tactlessness or worse may have contributed, is hard to say. Certainly the Freetown society found him harsh and overbearing.[3] MacCarthy, on the other hand, speaks of his 'eirenic actions and abilities', and his 'anxious desire to avoid animosities';[4] but quite an ill-tempered man could pass for eirenic if compared with Governor Sir Charles MacCarthy in a bad mood. In any case it is certain that the Freetown Methodists, who had so long conducted their own affairs, were not ready to submit at once, completely, and for ever to a pattern alien to their tradition and habits.

At any rate, before the end of 1816, hardly more than twenty months after Davies's arrival, he and the society had quarrelled irremediably. The society called him to answer to a charge of immorality. The evidence was supplied by a lady of dubious reputation, and no one seems to have taken it very seriously—indeed the charge seems to have been almost as much a formality as such charges in Athanasian times. When it came to the point, the society did not press it; but they did object to the attitudes and intemperance he displayed when confronted with it. A crisis of authority was reached: the leaders declared Davies suspended pending investigations. The missionary was indignant; and while the leaders were, according to Methodist discipline, still conducting their investigations, Davies took the case to the civil magistrates and was cleared.[5] It was now the leaders' turn to be indignant, and they refused any further ministrations from their

---

[1] Cf. MMS Archives, Davies to Fleming, 1 January 1817.

[2] MMS Archives, Brown to Entwistle, 31 March 1817.

[3] The missionary Samuel Brown speaks of Davies's 'self-confident zeal' (MMS Archives, 20 August 1818), and says that the basic objection of the society was to his 'temper' (ibid. 24 February 1817).

[4] MacCarthy to Davies, printed as an appendix to the *Journal*.

[5] MMS Archives, Brown to Entwistle, 31 March 1817. The CMS missionary Garnon speaks of the groundlessness of the charge (CMS Archives, CA 0126, 26 March 1817).

superintendent. The way in which Davies announces this is eloquent:

The leaders of the Society in Free Town have declared against me and have refused me the pulpit. I am *too plain* for them, and truly I have found them a proud stiff-necked generation. I understand they are going to accuse me of lording it over them, of being too proud for a Methodist preacher, and of paying too much attention to Government, the truth in this respect is, when we arrived here we found Methodism very low indeed, in the esteem of Government and the European Gentlemen in the Colony. My dear departed Jane's and my own conduct some how or other pleased the most respectable part of the Community, in consequent thereof some got jealous. As far as I can judge, most of our Leaders are of the American Republic spirit and are strongly averse to Government, I am a loyal subject to my King, and wish to do the little I can for the support of that Government especially in a foreign part where there are not so many able advocates as at home.[1]

And so they part, neither side understanding the other, each maintaining the Methodism they knew, yet each appearing in the other's eyes to be allied to things hateful to Methodism and pure religion.

Davies at once found employment under government as superintendent of the new recaptive village of Leopold; and the new missionary intended by London as Davies's assistant arrived to be his successor.

All this might pass for a storm in a small coffee cup, were it not that it was repeated. The Freetown Methodists had no wish to break with Conference: they gloried in the Methodist name, they wanted the European preacher. When the preacher arrived, however, the old tensions reappeared. Traditions moulded by Nova Scotia and Freetown marched uneasily with those moulded by English Methodism. In 1821 the superintendent of the day, John Huddleston, declared the society dissolved; and the Settler Methodist Church in Rawdon Street emerged as an entity independent of the mission.[2]

[1] MMS Archives, Davies to Fleming, 13 June 1817.
[2] Fyfe, *History of Sierra Leone*, pp. 139, 660.

To the missionaries this must have been almost a relief, and certainly no restriction, for they had plenty to do in the colony; the new population of recaptives seemed, and were, far more important for the future than were the settlers. In Freetown and the villages vigorous new societies sprang up under missionary guidance and leadership. The Maroons, for their part, soon became restive under what they felt to be settler arrogance, and formed their own church, on Methodist lines, and leased it for a fixed period to the Wesleyan mission. Alas, they, too, found missionary assumptions different from their own; and eventually a British superintendent marched out of the Maroon church shouting 'Your house is left unto you desolate', and the Maroon society, as the settler church had done, went its own way.[1]

The old societies, though small, and representing a declining community, made their own impact on the recaptives, who attended the settler churches just as they attended those of the missionaries. Here, again, communal tensions appeared. A recaptive might be converted; he might have spiritual gifts; he might hold a government job, marry a Nova Scotian wife, buy a house from an impoverished family of the settler aristocracy. But all this could not make him a settler: and this was symbolized when the gifted recaptive preacher Anthony O'Connor was kept as an auxiliary, confined to the lectern, refused the sanctified eminence of the pulpit of the settler chapel, in practice reserved to settler preachers. In 1844, the West African Methodist Church—as thoroughly Methodist in doctrine and polity as its antecedents—emerged, under O'Connor's leadership, from the bosom of settler Methodism. As missionary and settler parted, settler and Maroon and settler and recaptive parted likewise—all without any abandoment of the Methodist name, polity or practice.[2] Each community in Sierra Leone was radically affected by Christianity; the degree to which this transcended communial barriers should perhaps surprise us more than the frequency of ruptures.

And yet despite all this, Sierra Leone was the Morning Star of

[1] Ibid. pp. 139 f., 201, 660, 669.
[2] See C. H. Fyfe, 'The West African Methodists in the Nineteenth Century', *Sierra Leone Bulletin of Religion*, III (1961), 22–8.

Africa. The recaptives, uprooted from their own traditions, became in effect the first mass movement to Christianity in modern Africa. Furthermore, they became, in a matter of a generation, a large and highly mobile missionary force, with an effect right across West Africa and beyond it which passed anything Wilberforce could have envisaged.[1] All this was the fruit of the work of three agencies. First, of the European missionary force which struggled through the appalling mortality of the era of the White Man's Grave. Second, of the Christian settler community, which worked in its own way for the conversion of the newcomers,[2] and the extent of whose influence is hard to measure; for the new population adopted their ways and their revivalism entered the Christianity of the converted recaptives. Third, the determination and energy of a most remarkable colonial servant, Sir Charles MacCarthy, a man often distrusted by settlers and suspected by missionaries. Into the story of this movement, which could be held to have abundantly justified this Christian experiment, we cannot go; and long before it reached its crest, the principal characters in our story had departed. Davies, back in Wales, overwhelmed with depression, broke down and committed suicide;[3] MacCarthy's truncated corpse was left on the field at Bonsaso;

[1] On the development of Colony society see, e.g. J. E. Peterson, *Freetown: a Study of the Dynamics of Liberated African Society 1807–1870* (Ph.D. thesis, Northwestern University 1963; and now his book *Province of Freedom* (London 1969), chapters III–VII; A. T. Porter, *Creoledom* (London 1963). Its missionary contribution to West Africa has been both neglected and misread (cf. e.g. Stephen Neill, *Christian Missions* (London 1964), pp. 305 f.; R. S. Foster, *The Sierra Leone Church* (London 1961); but see P. E. H. Hair, *The early study of Nigerian Languages* (Cambridge 1967); 'CMS "Native Clergy" in West Africa to 1900', *Sierra Leone Bulletin of Religion*, IV (1962), 71–2; 'Freetown Christianity and Africa', ibid. VI (1964), 13–21; 'Niger languages and Sierra Leone missionary linguists', *Bulletin of the Society for African Church History*, II (1966), 127–38; cf. also J. H. Kopytoff, *A Preface to modern Nigeria: the 'Sierra Leonians' in Yoruba, 1830–1890* (Madison 1965).

[2] It is clear that early missionaries in the Colony saw Nova Scotian evangelists as effective rivals in recaptive villages: cf. of many, CMS Archives, CA 0126, Garnon to Pratt, 26 March 1817: 'Now I see the need of your throwing all your strength into the Colony, so that each town may be possess'd by us, otherwise not only Mr Davies but a sad mongrel set of Baptists etc. will get there.'

[3] See *Dictionary of Welsh Biography*, ad loc.

and as for the leaders of the settler Methodists, some people in Freetown believed that their indignant shades made a characteristic return to earth in 1861, when their successors at Rawdon Street reunited with the Wesleyan Methodist Mission.[1] It is at least unquestionable that in that year the chapel fell down.

[1] For the reconciliation, collapse of the building, and the rationale offered by some, see C. Marke, *Origins of Wesleyan Methodism in Sierra Leone*, pp. 113 ff.

THE SELECTION AND TRAINING OF
MISSIONARIES IN THE EARLY
NINETEENTH CENTURY

by PETER HINCHLIFF

ANYONE who studies the techniques and strategy of early nineteenth-century missionaries and (even more) of early nineteenth-century missionary societies can hardly avoid gaining the impression that they suffered from a romantic casualness. It is as if zealous Christians of the period were so convinced that the Lord would guide and provide for the missionary that he really did not need much mundane preparation. Nineteenth-century missionaries often simply disappeared into bush, desert or jungle, stopped when they came to a site where there was food, water and heathen, and preached in whatever language happened to be available.

Having said this, one must immediately qualify one's judgement. Nineteenth-century missions were remarkably successful, so one must not be too cynical about them. The contribution made to the study of languages and of the religious and social customs of people outside Europe, by men like William Carey and his companions in Serampore, is well known and can be paralleled in many parts of the world. Some of the missionary societies, too, could be extremely efficient. The London Missionary Society, for instance, had miniature portraits painted of all its missionaries to serve the sort of purpose for which we today would use a passport photograph.[1] The Methodist Missionary Society kept a direct and, at times frustratingly detailed, financial control over their agents in the field.[2] Moreover, I am chiefly familiar with missionary affairs in South Africa, and it may well

---

[1] Some of these portraits still survive and are kept in the society's archives.
[2] See e.g. letter from J. Whitworth, dated 8 April 1826, defending himself against charges of 'unjustifiable expenditure'—the Methodist Missionary Society Archives, London, Box IV—Cape, File 1826.

be that they are not at all typical of what was happening elsewhere.

So far as South Africa is concerned, the picture which emerges seems to indicate that both the selection and the training of early missionaries was extremely haphazard. The very first real missionary in the subcontinent was a Moravian who was given the job, and sent off absolutely alone, as a penance for the sin of apostasy.[1] The Moravian principle that every missionary must have a trade so as to be able to teach his converts to work with their hands and to make the mission self-supporting was, of course, excellent and very Pauline. It did not always work very well in the unimaginably primitive conditions of the African veld. To be a bricklayer, cutler or blacksmith presupposes the prior existence of bricks, steel and horses.

The first LMS missionary to South Africa, Vanderkemp, selected himself in much the same casual way. His initial letter to the society speaks of his burning desire to be a missionary, and his sense of vocation to work either in Persia or at the Cape, and then adds 'but I have no knowledge of Persian'.[2] It is true that he had many other, more positive, qualifications for working at the Cape, and that he himself several times set out the sort of qualities and standards to be required from other intending missionaries.[3] The society considered many candidates, from whom they selected three to accompany Vanderkemp, and proudly wrote to tell him the result. These three were described as missionary students. One of them is to be encouraged to continue his studies—in spelling.[4]

Many of the early missionaries were, indeed, barely literate. This does not, of course, mean that they were the less devoted or noble, but it does mean that such instruction as they were given was in the elements of reading and writing, rather than

[1] B. Krüger, *Genadendal and its Satellites* (unpublished Ph.D. thesis, Rhodes University, Grahamstown, 1965), pp. 15 f.
[2] London Missionary Society Archives, Box 1, Folder 1, Jacket A, J. T. Vanderkemp, 26 July 1797.
[3] See also the society's undated instructions to Vanderkemp in the same jacket.
[4] London Missionary Society Archives, Box 1, Folder 1, Jacket C., T. Haweis, 22 February 1799.

in specifically missionary preparation. The same seems to hold true at all levels, even where the candidates were already literate. An Anglican shop assistant called Steabler wrote to the SPG in 1846, offering himself as a missionary and asking what training was necessary.[1] Unfortunately we do not know what reply he received, but six weeks later Steabler wrote again, giving an account of his private studies and asking about St Augustine's College, Canterbury.[2] Whatever training he had, it cannot have been either lengthy or specialized, for not much more than a year later he was at work in Natal as a deacon. A recent article on Philip Quaque and West Africa shows, too, that even in very special (and optimum) conditions little was done to prepare missionaries for the particular circumstances they would be likely to find.[3] They were trained, at best, as if they were going to be English country parsons—at worst, as if anything would do for mission work.

Only the Scots, perhaps not surprisingly, seem to have tackled the problem systematically.[4] After some early unhappy experiences with ill-educated missionaries, standards were made very high and the same theological training was prescribed for intending missionaries as for prospective parish ministers.[5] This well-intentioned rule was itself to cause trouble later, when there was a furious controversy over whether to train African ordinands in Greek, Latin and mathematics, or on some pattern better suited to conditions in the country at the time.[6]

Little wonder, then, that in spite of efforts to persuade missionaries to adopt a different approach,[7] they often preached

[1] United Society for the Propagation of the Gospel Archives, South Africa—Box 2, Folder 32, W. A. Steabler, 9 September 1846.
[2] Ibid. W. A. Steabler, 21 October 1846.
[3] Muriel Bentley, 'Philip Quaque', *Church Quarterly Review*, CLXVII (April–June 1966), 151 f.
[4] For the early, and comparatively enlightened, rules of the Glasgow Missionary Society relating to the selection of missionaries, their training and qualifications, see *Glasgow Missionary Society Quarterly Paper* (June 1828), pp. 3 f.
[5] R. H. W. Shepherd, *Lovedale, South Africa, 1841–1941* (Lovedale 1941), p. 29.
[6] Ibid. pp. 153 f.
[7] See the regulations of the Glasgow Missionary Society referred to above, and those of Bishop Cotterill of Grahamstown in C. Lewis and G. E. Edwards, *Historical Records of the Church of the Province of S. Africa*, SPCK (London 1934), p. 263.

through an interpreter (who was frequently perforce not a Christian), and delivered themselves of almost exactly the same kind of sermons as they might have preached in the pulpits of England.

It may be worth quoting an early missionary's description of his technique. A Methodist, John Ayliff, wrote in his diary on Tuesday 9 November 1830:

The plan I adopted in order to get their attention fixed was, when I saw any of the men sitting at the kraals conversing together, to make a sudden appearance among them and suddenly saying I have brought you today the Word of God—then they would reply, Well what does the Word of God say. This would open my way to address them. Some during the time I would be speaking would appear to express their Astonishment, others their Contempt. Either by Speaking to Each other or Laughing quite loud...

Sometimes questions of a very pertinent nature would be asked, as during the whole of this Itinerary the Subject of preaching has been the Soul's immortality and a Future State of Rewards & punishments and the Love of God in Christ to man. They would ask when did *we* get a Soul—will the Soul always live—what are we now to do, since you tell us these things. Tho' these questions were asked, yet I felt no reason to believe that they were indications of any concern on their part to save their Souls.[1]

It is not part of my purpose to decry the missionaries, to minimize their achievements or what they suffered. Ayliff was one of the great Methodist pioneers in southern Africa. He was in no sense a well-educated man but, like many early Methodist missionaries, he kept up his reading, faithfully doing what John Wesley had hoped that his preachers would do. It was, no doubt, inevitable that such men should have very little knowledge of the language, customs, and beliefs of the people to whom they preached. Even the great Robert Moffat, after twenty years in South Africa, could declare that the aboriginal peoples of the subcontinent had absolutely no religion at all.[2] Of course, if one

[1] Ayliff's *Diary*, Government Archives, Cape Town, Acc. 80/1.
[2] Robert Moffat, *Missionary Labours and Scenes in South Africa* (London 1842), p. 243.

defines 'heathenism' in a certain way (priests in plumes and vestments, idols decorated with precious stones, the elaborate ritual of sacrifice), then one might assume that traditional African beliefs were not really a religion. And magic and witchcraft were so difficult to handle because one did not know whether to treat them as satanic or as imaginary! What is strange is that, though the missionaries came in time to lay much of the foundations of modern linguistic and anthropological studies, the societies did so little to incorporate these things in their training courses.

Perhaps the real importance of these few facts about the selection and training of missionaries in one part of the world is this: that it reveals how much work remains to be done in the field of missionary history. Most works in this field are either a mass of dull detail, or congratulatory volumes on the glorious triumphs of the Gospel. Very little thoroughly digested assessment of policy, strategy or technique has ever been attempted. It used to be fashionable to eulogize the missionaries. It is becoming the fashion to sneer at them. One thing that is badly needed is a critical study of the societies, how they chose and trained their men, and how much help they gave them in the field, what was done to plan strategy systematically, and how much real knowledge headquarters possessed about the conditions obtaining on the actual mission stations.

THE CHURCH'S RESPONSE TO THE CHOLERA OUTBREAK OF 1866

by G. HUELIN

THE publication of Mr Norman Longmate's book *King Cholera* in November 1966 served as a reminder of the terrible scourge which afflicted this country on no less than four separate occasions during the nineteenth century. While this volume was, no doubt—as the 'blurb' on its dust-jacket affirms—'an important contribution to social history', so far as the part which the Church played during those critical years, the half was not told in its pages. In this short paper it will be my task to try to repair this omission in regard to just one of the four major outbreaks of the disease in England, the last in fact, that of the year 1866; and to say something of the response made by churchmen and women to the cholera outbreak of a century ago.

The cholera of 1866 seems to have made its first appearance in this country at Southampton, whither it was brought by a ship from Alexandria.[1] As on the three previous occasions the disease soon became fairly widespread, although one or two areas were to be the main victims: among them Liverpool and, above all, east London.

In May 1866 emigrants from a boat, the *Helvetia*, which had docked at Liverpool, some of them cholera suspects, were confined in the local workhouse, and thus the town's population escaped the disease. By the end of May all traces of cholera had disappeared from the workhouse; it seemed indeed to have been effectively stamped out as far as Liverpool was concerned. However, in the month of July it was to return to take its toll of some two thousand lives.[2]

At this period Liverpool still formed part of the diocese of

---

[1] N. Longmate, *King Cholera* (London 1966), pp. 212–13.

[2] *Liverpool Daily Post* 4, 10, 15 and 29 May, and 17 July. (Unless otherwise indicated, newspapers referred to are of the year 1866).

Chester, whose bishop was William Jacobson. So bad had the cholera outbreak become that on Sunday 26 August at the church of St Martin-in-the-Fields in Liverpool, Bishop Jacobson preached twice on behalf of the afflicted families to crowded congregations and drew from these collections of £26. His text in the morning was Phil. i. 21 and in the evening Job xxxiii. 14. In the course of the evening sermon the bishop took the opportunity to comment strongly on the evils of drunkenness as being particularly conducive to the pestilence, and to urge the need for sanitary improvements.[1] St Martin's was noted for its ritualistic practices, and attached to it was a community of Sisters who then had charge of a small temporary cholera hospital adjoining the church. Between the morning and evening services Bishop Jacobson visited the hospital, and in its principal ward offered prayers and gave his blessing. The reaction of certain of the Liverpool Orangemen showed itself when it came to the bishop's departure after Evensong. These men followed his carriage crying 'Down with the old Puseyite bishop', some opening the doors and even attempting to smash the windows.[2] Dean Burgon in his *Lives of Twelve Good Men* has left a note of the incident:

Did you ever hear of the Bishop, with that devotion to duty which was so intense, and so utterly without show, going to visit the cholera huts in the suburbs of Liverpool? The carriage in which he was, was pelted with mud by the Orange mob, because 'sisters' were in charge of the huts. He never spoke one word of annoyance. 'It is all in the day's work'—'We must take it as it comes'.[3]

London, where the number of cholera deaths during 1866 amounted to nearly eight thousand, received the germ in the first instance from a most extraordinary source: namely, a farm situated at Theydon Bois in Essex. Thence the disease travelled down the valley of the river Lea to the poor and overcrowded districts of the eastern quarters of the capital where it soon caused great havoc.[4]

[1] Ibid. 27 August.   [2] Ibid. 30 August.
[3] J. W. Burgon, *Lives of Twelve Good Men* (London 1891, one-volume edition), p. 388.
[4] N. Longmate, *King Cholera*, p. 212; R. T. Davidson and W. Benham, *Archibald Campbell Tait* (1891), I, 470.

Possibly owing to the ritualist troubles in which he was then involved, the work of Archibald Campbell Tait, who was Bishop of London at the time of the last cholera outbreak, has been largely overlooked. Despite the fact that in the spring of that year Tait had been seriously ill, on receiving news of the arrival of cholera he immediately abandoned his holiday plans in order to devote himself to the pressing problems which this created for his diocese. As to these, he was later to write: 'The state of things in the East of London became very bad indeed. The whole district which had any connection with the river Lea was infected. I summoned a meeting of the clergy of Bethnal Green, Stepney and Spitalfields, and we endeavoured to make arrangements which might aid the sanitary authorities.' The bishop took the lead in organizing financial relief for the sufferers, and a letter from him to *The Times* produced £3,000 within twenty-four hours.[1] One August Sunday, accompanied by his wife, he paid personal visits to the cholera hospitals in the parishes of St George's-in-the-East and Wapping. There he showed a keen interest in all that was being done, and offered prayers in the hospital wards.[2] The newspapers in reporting this, declared that the bishop had spent Sunday 'in true Apostolic fashion'.[3] On another occasion he went to one of the poorest districts in east London, St James's, Ratcliff, where the cholera was particularly prevalent and fatal.[4] Here he tried to cheer the convalescents gathered in the schoolroom adjoining the church, many of whom were so weak as scarcely to be able to stand. The bishop also visited the various cholera hospitals run by members of the Religious Communities, including that under the charge of Miss Sellon at Spitalfields, where he went through the wards speaking to the patients.[5]

A similar heroism and complete absence of self-interest or thought of self-preservation was shown by many of the parish clergy. In 1866 John Richard Green, author of *A Short History of the English People*, was appointed incumbent of St Philip's,

[1] R. Davidson and W. Benham, *Archibald Campbell Tait*, p. 470 and footnote.
[2] *Church Times*, 25 August.   [3] *Liverpool Daily Post*, 21 August.
[4] *The Times*, 5 September.   [5] *Church Times*, 15 September.

Stepney. Shortly afterwards, the cholera broke out in his parish, and Green devoted himself unsparingly to his duties. A contributor to the *Fortnightly Review* later said of him:

Within an hour from the first seizure in his parish, Green himself met the dying patients in the London Hospital and thenceforward while the plague lasted, Green, like other clergy in the parishes attacked, worked day and night amidst the panic-stricken people, as Officer of Health, Inspector of Nuisances, Ambulance Superintendent, as well as spiritual consoler and burier of the dead. His only dread was for his friends. He almost burst into passion when he met the wife of a neighbouring clergyman visiting, like himself, the sick of her parish in the London Hospital. He implored her, for her children's sake, to withdraw from such a post of danger, and only acquiesced in her remaining upon seeing how her presence steadied the overwrought and frightened nurses.[1]

One of Green's closest friends, the Rev. H. R. Haweis, then curate in a West End parish, went to Stepney to help in ministering to the sick and dying. Haweis records how very often neither Green nor himself undressed at night, but slept on a sofa ready for any emergency. He also mentions the fact that the only people who seemed willing to help Green were the lowest women of the town, and that it was no uncommon sight to see him going to an infected house accompanied by a couple of social outcasts. On one occasion he discovered a man dangerously ill with cholera in the upstairs room of a house. Some draymen in the street below refused to give him assistance. Green therefore resolved to carry the man downstairs alone, but his slight frame was unequal to the strain, and both men fell from top to bottom.[2]

At the end of June 1866, Charles Lowder became the first vicar of the newly consecrated church of St Peter's, London Docks. About a fortnight later there occurred in the parish a slight case of cholera: it was a foretaste of things to come. No better description can be given of the conditions which here, as in other places, afforded an ideal breeding-ground for the disease, than that written by Lowder himself:

[1] P. L. Gell in *Fortnightly Review*, May 1883.
[2] H. R. Haweis in *Contemporary Review*, May 1883.

It can be no wonder that in such districts as ours, where there is at all times so much poverty and distress; where the drainage was as yet untouched by the improvements made in other parts; where our poor are so crowded from want of house-room; where the alleys are so close, and the sanitary arrangements very defective; where, during the hottest part of the season, we had fermenting amongst us a large manure manufactory, in which was collected, in a very mountain of impurity, hundreds of tons of the very refuse of the streets, the stinking sweepings of the market, rotten fish, oranges, etc., to be mixed up and then carted off to barges in the river—it can, I say, be no wonder that when the cholera once broke out amongst us it should have proved most fatal.[1]

Night and day Lowder toiled with his brother clergy to fight the disease. He wrote letters to *The Times* telling of how members of his congregation had died: one within nineteen, the other within twelve, hours of being attacked by cholera; and of how in one family alone, six children were left as orphans. He appealed for brandy, wine, clothes and bedding, and, above all, for money:[2] and the response was such that he was able to open a home at Seaford for patients convalescing after their recovery from the disease. A contemporary, Dr Andrew Clark, physician to the London Hospital, referred to Lowder as 'one of the most active and useful men in the east end of London'.[3] Today, in St Peter's Church, one of the panels in a modern window commemorating Lowder's life and work depicts him as carrying in his arms a sick child on the way to the cholera hospital. Small wonder that he earned the name of 'Father' Lowder—the first Anglican priest, it is said, ever to be addressed in this way.

Because of reports he had received, Dr E. B. Pusey decided to forgo the peace of the Long Vacation at Oxford to journey to London, where he took lodgings in City Road in order to see if he might be of use in tending cholera victims. He found more than enough to occupy his time: so much so, in fact, that though he had planned to stay for only a week, he was still there in October. Pusey divided his time between working in the British

[1] (M. Trench), *Charles Lowder*, p. 218.
[2] *The Times*, 28 July.   [3] Ibid. 4 September.

Museum Reading Room on his *Answer to Newman*, and sick-visiting in Spitalfields and the neighbourhood. Dr Sutton, the physician at the cholera hospital which Miss Sellon had recently opened in the Spitalfields area, was experiencing difficulty in persuading the Jewish patients to do what was required of them. Pusey, who was Regius Professor of Hebrew at Oxford, spoke to them in their own language and was completely successful.[1] Later, a friend recorded that Dr Pusey 'had reduced himself to only one pair of shoes, and those so full of holes that one very wet day it really was impossible for him to go out'.[2] Nor were Pusey's ministrations limited to Spitalfields. The rector of Bethnal Green, who was not only fully immersed in his parochial duties but also those of the Vestry of which he was chairman, to his surprise one morning received a visit from the Oxford don who carried with him a letter of introduction from the Bishop of London. He had come, he said, to act as curate and to attend to the needs of the parishioners. 'And', says the rector, 'he did so quietly and unobtrusively this true gentleman, this humble servant of Christ, assisted me in this most trying duty of visiting the plague-stricken homes of the poor of Bethnal Green.'[3]

A few clergy gave help of a different kind. The Rev. E. F. Whitehouse, vicar of Saltney in Cheshire, when taking the chair at a public meeting held in the town for the purpose of considering the best means of preventing the spread of the disease in the district, proffered the sound advice to people not to use various recipes supposed to cure cholera which were then appearing in the newspapers in great numbers. Rather, he said, they should in case of need consult a medical practitioner, since serious and fatal results were often brought about by reliance upon quacks.[4] The Rev. Francis Pigou, incumbent of St Philip's Chapel, Regent Street, London, advertised a sermon which he had preached entitled *Sowing and Reaping*, price 6d.: the proceeds to be given to the cholera fund of the Metropolitan Visiting and Relief Association.[5] Finally, a clergyman whose name remains unknown,

[1] H. P. Liddon, *Life of Edward Bouverie Pusey* (1897), v, 141–2.
[2] J. G. Lockhart, *Charles Lindley Viscount Halifax*, I, 136.
[3] H. P. Liddon, *Life of Edward Bouverie Pusey*, v, 142–3.
[4] *Chester Chronicle*, 11 August.   [5] *Guardian*, 15 August.

expressed his opinion that all those who were 'under fire' deserved an extra chop and glass of stout a day, and backed it up by sending the sum of £10 to be divided into grants of £1 each to the men who were working in infected districts.[1]

No doubt, as in every epidemic of this nature, there were some clergy who deserted their posts or displayed cowardice. Even so, there is a touch of malicious gossip or nineteenth-century party strife in the *Church Times* report of the time which pictures a clergyman (needless to say, Protestant in his sympathies) standing outside the door of the workhouse cholera ward, with a bag of camphor to avoid infection, and having knelt there on his outspread pocket-handkerchief and said an extempore prayer, hastily retiring; while the Anglo-Catholic priest fearlessly attends the bedside of the patient who has sought spiritual help, and gives her absolution.[2] Fortunately, even if this instance of failure of clerical duty be true, few cases of the kind have been recorded. Indeed, when paying a visit to the East End at the beginning of September 1866 in order to confer with the local clergy as to the best means of providing for cholera orphans and convalescents, the Bishop of London could pay tribute to the magnificent work done there, and could declare that the thanks of all was due to the clergy who at the risk of their own health and life had laboured to minister to the physical and spiritual needs of their people.[3]

Others, of course, besides the clergy of the Established Church had their share both in the ministrations and in personal loss and suffering. In the Liverpool outbreak Father Callaghan, parish priest of the Eldon Street Roman Catholic Church, died through catching the cholera while visiting his sick people.[4] The Roman Catholic Bishop of Liverpool, Dr Goss, announced a three months' suspension of the rules concerning fasting and abstinence.[5] Archbishop Manning sent a circular letter to the clergy in the poorer districts of the diocese of Westminster, requesting them to use their influence to prevent 'wakes', or assemblies at funerals of more than the number of persons actually required.[6]

[1] Ibid. 22 August.
[2] *Church Times*, 4 August.
[3] *The Times*, 1 September.
[4] Ibid. 15 May.
[5] *Liverpool Daily Post*, 6 August.
[6] *The Times*, 13 August.

The Methodist Recorder, in a leading article, urged as the best weapons to combat the cholera 'a clean life, a good conscience, a healthy body and a courageous soul';[1] and it noted that Methodist ministers in London's East End were working together with others in house-to-house visiting, and in distributing relief from the Lord Mayor's Fund.[2] Similarly, the Congregational ministers set up a committee to see what relief they could give to a number of urgent cases which had been brought to their notice by their evangelists at work in east London.[3] In Spitalfields, some young members of the Society of Friends undertook the management of an invalid-kitchen to provide well-cooked and nourishing food, which they distributed freely to the sick as far as their resources would allow.[4] One of the agents of the London City Mission working in Whitechapel died of cholera.[5]

Many people at this period were highly suspicious of the Religious Communities of the Church of England; and this, in spite of the gallant part which some of the Sisters had played in previous cholera epidemics. In Liverpool especially, religious bigotry still showed itself in 1866. Reference has already been made to the reception given to the Bishop of Chester, William Jacobson, in consequence of his visit to St Martin's Church and his recognition of the work done there on behalf of the cholera patients by the Sisters of Mercy. Earlier, the incumbent of St Martin's, the Rev. Cecil Wray, had offered the services of the newly established sisterhood to the Special Cholera Committee. The committee members replied, coldly declining this offer on the grounds that the Sisters might be led to indulge in proselytizing among the patients.[6] Despite this rebuff, the St Martin's Sisters put to good use some huts adjoining their church. If the recollections of a former Liverpool resident, Miss Buxton, are accurate, their courage cost them their lives: for she seems to recall that the entire staff of St Martin's, clergy and sisters, was wiped out by the epidemic.[7]

[1] *Methodist Recorder*, 10 August. [2] Ibid. 24 August.
[3] *Guardian*, 22 August. [4] *The Times*, 13 August.
[5] *Guardian*, 22 August. [6] *Church Times*, 4 August.
[7] Miss I. Buxton, in a private communication to me.

Criticism of the Religious Communities was, however, soon to be silenced. In London, the 1866 cholera outbreak had the effect of finally breaking down the opposition to the various sisterhoods at work in the metropolis. Writing in her *Memories of a Sister of St Saviour's Priory* at Haggerston, Mother Kate sums up the situation briefly when she says: 'The visitation of the cholera was the key which opened the door of many a house, and many a heart which dwelt inside it to us.' Again, one of the Sisters of the Holy Cross, attached to St Peter's, London Docks, a Community which was long to be remembered in the tough neighbourhood for its acts of herosim and self-sacrifice, remarked 'We never had any trouble after the cholera'.[1]

During the month of August Miss Lydia Sellon, the Mother Superior of the Devonport Sisters of Mercy, who had already had experience of the cholera some years earlier at Plymouth, took over a large unused warehouse in Commercial Street in the Spitalfields district of London. Here she fitted up several floors as wards for men, women and children. In all, the hospital could accommodate about two hundred patients. Sisters from Haggerston, Osnaburgh Street, Ascot, and Oxford helped her in the task of nursing.[2] Charles Grafton, later to become Bishop of Fond du Lac, agreed at the suggestion of Pusey to be voluntary chaplain to Miss Sellon's hospital. Part of his task was to get the sick and poor of the neighbourhood into the hospital; and for this purpose he used what he called our 'cholera-cab'. On one occasion he went to a near-by thieves' den, and was welcomed with the invitation, 'Don't be afraid to come in: we are all honest thieves down here'.[3]

A marked increase in the number of cholera victims in the north London area during the autumn of 1866 gave Dr Walter Rickards, resident physician of University College Hospital, in making an appeal for financial aid through the columns of *The Times*, the opportunity of testifying to the work of yet another of the religious communities, that of All Saints. His letter revealed

---

[1] (M. Trench), *Charles Lowder*, 227.
[2] T. J. Williams, *Priscilla Lydia Sellon*, 228.
[3] C. C. Grafton, *A Journey Godward*, 41–3.

that not only had the valuable services of the Mother Superior and the Sisters of All Saints' Home for long been appreciated in the management of nursing at the hospital, but also that many of the staff nurses, who were then busily engaged in tending cholera patients, owed their entire training and education to the Community.[1]

Finally, something must be said of the work undertaken by Christian laymen and women, the results of which were in some cases to last for many years to come.

One young man who was first brought into contact with slum conditions through the cholera outbreak of 1866, and whose entire outlook as a Christian was to be influenced by his experiences of that year, was Charles Wood, later Viscount Halifax. News had reached him through a clerical friend of the distress among the families of those dying of the cholera, and he decided to journey to London to see if he could be of any use. One of his first visits was to a Stepney family in company with the curate of St Philip's. His main contribution, however, was at Miss Sellon's hospital in Spitalfields where he acted as honorary secretary, and was able to render good service in looking after the staff, paying wages, sending messages and arranging funerals.[2] This hospital also owed much to another layman, Edward Palmer, one of the directors of the Bank of England, who not only contributed large sums of money, but allowed his wife to share in the task of nursing.[3]

At the London Hospital Thomas Barnardo, then a student training as a medical missionary for work in China, volunteered his services to combat the cholera. To the young and enthusiastic Barnardo, it seemed that the visitation had tended to make people more serious; and he used the opportunity to distribute copies of the Scriptures in street-markets and public-houses. What particularly impressed him was the appalling number of child-victims: a factor which was to lead him in later days to found the Homes by which he is still remembered.[4]

[1] *The Times*, 28 September.
[2] J. G. Lockhart, *Charles Lindley Viscount Halifax*, I, 132 ff.
[3] C. C. Grafton, *A Journey Godward*, 42.
[4] A. E. Williams, *Barnardo of Stepney*, p. 61; N. Longmate, *King Cholera*, 222.

Mention has already been made of the efforts of A. C. Tait, then Bishop of London. His wife Catherine was to play a part in the crisis scarcely less noteworthy. Not only did she very often accompany her husband on his visits to the suffering, but together with two women friends, Catherine Gladstone and Catherine Marsh—the triumvirate earned the nickname of the 'three Catherines'—she helped in establishing more permanent institutions.

With the name of Catherine Tait was to be associated a house opened in Fulham to accommodate small girls who had become orphans as a result of the cholera. Subsequently, the orphanage was transferred to the parish of St Peter's in the isle of Thanet, where a new building was erected on land given by Catherine's husband, who had now become Archbishop of Canterbury. So there came into being the 'St Peter's Orphan and Convalescent Homes'.[1]

Catherine Gladstone, whose medical skill her husband once praised, threw herself day after day into the work of the London Hospital, regardless of the filth, the smells, or the danger of infection. A devout churchgoer, she comforted many of the dying with the assurance that she would personally be responsible for the care of their children. Frequently, she was to be seen carrying a baby from the hospital wrapped only in a blanket, his own clothes having been burned for fear of infection. He was on his way to the orphanage for boys which she started at Hawarden. Another offshoot of the cholera epidemic was 'Mrs Gladstone's Free Convalescent Home for the Poor' at Woodford.[2]

Catherine Marsh, the daughter of an Anglican clergyman, also gave her services to the London Hospital. Some of the scenes which she witnessed there were to provide an illustration in *Death and Life*—one of her numerous religious tracts which appeared in print: for, like others, Miss Marsh hoped that the cholera might serve as a means of conversion. With the help of friends she set up a convalescent home for patients unfit to return to their own families. This began its life in two cottages,

---

[1] R. Davidson and W. Benham, *Archibald Campbell Tait*, I, 471.
[2] G. Battiscombe, *Mrs Gladstone*, pp. 131 ff.

lent by Sir Thomas Fowell Buxton, M.P., on his estate close to Epping Forest in Essex. When the necessary funds had been raised, it was transferred to Blackrock, Brighton, to serve as a convalescent home close to the Sussex Downs and facing the sea. Eventually, it was moved to Worthing, where it continued to fulfil its good purpose until the outbreak of the Second World War in 1939.[1]

The year 1866 witnessed the fourth and last of the nineteenth-century cholera outbreaks in England. Once again, as on earlier occasions, the Church responded to the crisis; and the part played in that response by men such as Archibald Campbell Tait, John Richard Green and Charles Lowder, deserves to be more widely known than has hitherto been the case. But it was the response made by Christian women of the time which earns even higher praise, as Tait, then Bishop of London, clearly recognized when, in December of that year, in delivering his Charge to the clergy of the diocese he said:

I should be false to all good feeling if I did not publicly testify to the great help which London received, during the late appalling sickness, from the self-denying efforts of Christian women—some acting alone, on the impulse of their own individual generous nature, some living in communities, of which it is the common bond to be ready, for Christ's sake, to tend the poor, at whatever risk. Our cholera hospitals, the crowded streets and squalid homes of our east end parishes, were cheered and blessed by the presence of many true Sisters of Mercy of the Church of England, without whom it is certain that in those desolate regions the suffering would have been far worse than it was.[2]

[1] Miss M. O'Rorke in a private communication to me. See also L. E. O'Rorke, *Life and Friendships of Catherine Marsh*.
[2] A. C. Tait, *Charge to the Clergy of the Diocese of London*, December 1866.

THE HISTORY OF MISSIONS: AN ACADEMIC DISCIPLINE

by S. C. NEILL

INTRODUCTION

EVERYONE knows that the Christian world mission exists. Not everyone would be prepared to agree that the mission should be regarded as a fit subject for academic study.

There is an interesting difference in the manner in which this question has been dealt with in Germany, in the United States, and in Britain.

The Germans are the great theorists; it is not surprising that Germany was the first country to develop a full-scale theory of missions and to invent the unpleasing hybrid 'missiology'. The first plan for academic teaching of missiology came from Karl Graul, director of the Leipzig mission, who in 1864 drew up a plan for such teaching in the university of Erlangen, and had actually delivered an admired introductory lecture on the subject. His early death made impossible the realization of the plans that he had drawn up. The first full-time professor of missions was Gustav Warneck, whose immense *Missionslehre* began to appear in 1897, the year in which its author was appointed as professor in the old pietistic university of Halle. Warneck the theorist was followed by the historian Julius Richter in Berlin. Richter was a typically German toiler, whose volumes on various regions of the earth are full of minutely accurate information, a little marred by the all too obvious view of the writer that only Germans understand how to carry out the task of mission, and that the British have never done anything but make mistakes in the political as well as in the religious field.

At the present time there are five full-scale professorships of missions in the Protestant faculties of Western Germany. There will shortly be six, as the new faculty at Munich plans to include a chair of missions and shortly to make an appointment. To these must be added the professorship still in existence at Halle in Eastern Germany, where Professor Arno Lehmann continues to bring forth fascinating material from the archives of the old Danish-Halle mission; and the Roman Catholic professorship at Münster held by Josef Glazik, to whom we owe two exceptionally good books on the missions of the Orthodox Churches.

In the United States professors of missions are a remarkably numerous species. Almost all the major seminaries of the Protestant churches have chairs of missions, and the professors are linked in a number of regional associations. In many cases these chairs are held by retired missionaries—an arrangement which is very nice for the retired missionaries, perhaps less so for the students whose expectations in the matter of academic standards are not always fully met.

In the United Kingdom to this day there is not a single full-time professorship of missions. Professor Myklebust of Oslo, in his immense work *The study of Missions in Theological Education* (Oslo 1957), commenting on this 'Continued non-recognition of Missions as a Separate Subject of Study', kindly attributes this not so much to neglect as to a different point of view—the study of missions will gain not by the founding of new chairs or the introduction of new courses, but by the reorientation of all theological teaching to those wider horizons which the missionary enterprise represents. He quotes Bishop E. R. Morgan as having written in 1928:

All the teaching given at all Theological Colleges, not merely those training missionaries for work overseas, needs to be orientated with a view to drawing out, by comparison with other attempts to come to terms with reality, the essential uniqueness and power of Christianity as the way of salvation for the whole world.[1]

This is a view which I shall be concerned to defend later in this lecture. It is, however, not clear whether the desired orientation has actually taken place in the last forty years. 'Continued non-recognition' is the rule in British universities and other places of religion and sound learning.

[1] E. R. Morgan (ed.), *Essays Catholic and missionary*, p. 248.

But, whatever the method followed, the end-result appears to have been the same. Few, except the experts in missions themselves, have come to the point of taking this study seriously as a necessary part of the theological encyclopaedia. The study of missions has remained marginal, and only grudgingly accepted. In at least one German faculty the professor of missions is continually re-elected as dean by his colleagues, on the ground presumably that he really has nothing important to do. Students avoid lectures in this field, if they can. If constrained to attend 'required courses', they complain that they are boring and irrelevant, a troublesome distraction from what they regard as their 'scientific studies'.

WHAT HAS GONE WRONG?

If this is the situation, it must be admitted that the representatives of the missionary cause are themselves to some extent responsible. The greater part of the missionary literature produced in the nineteenth century suffers from three grave defects.

In the first place, it is written largely in terms of missionary societies and in connection with their special interests. This means that a vast amount is included which cannot be of any interest to either historian or theologian as such. There are exceptions. Eugene Stock's three-volume history of the Church Missionary Society takes a broad view of Church history, and contains valuable information on a vast variety of topics. But the society interest is still central even in this particularly valuable work.

Secondly, almost all this writing is hagiographical and edifying. For this there are a variety of reasons. Relations and friends of persons referred to were still living at the time of writing, and offence had to be avoided. There was a natural desire, when so much real heroism and goodness were present, to touch up the narratives a little, and to suppress the shadows which in point of fact would have added so much life to the page. The missionaries really made far more mistakes than was generally admitted, and had many more faults to balance their virtues. But the desire to make a good impression sometimes carried more weight than a strict regard for truth.

Thirdly, much of this writing failed to set the events recorded in the frame of contemporary history. Some great events, naturally, made their influence felt even in these somewhat secluded lives. It was impossible to write about India in the middle of the nineteenth century without some reference to what was then called by everyone the Indian Mutiny and its influence on missionary affairs. But, perhaps because the events were too recent for the perspective to be fully grasped, missionary history seemed to be treated as a special world of its own, almost wholly unrelated to the life of the larger and less sacred world around it.

On the other side, account has to be taken of the manner in which Church history has been taught in a great many institutions of learning. In general, it has been presented as the history of the Church, which always seems to me a very boring subject.

An immense amount of time has been spent on the theological controversies by which the Church has been afflicted—a story which is not without importance, but belongs rather to the history of Christian doctrine than to the story of the Church as such.

Almost all Church history has been presented exclusively from the western point of view. After Chalcedon in 451, the eastern Churches simply cease to exist. As the present Master of Selwyn has pointed out, Newman seems to have depended for such knowledge of Byzantium as he possessed almost exclusively on Gibbon, not the best possible *cicerone* for that part of the Christian world. This defect, it must be admitted, is in process of correction through the heroic labours of such writers as Sir Steven Runciman and Fr Joseph Gill, and partly also because the Orthodox Churches are no longer a distant reality somewhere on the margin of consciousness, but a present fact, especially in the United States, where Orthodox Christians are as numerous as Jews, and are ever more vocally laying claim to recognition as the fourth estate, along with Catholics, Protestants and Jews.

But account is hardly ever taken of what since the publication of Professor K. S. Latourette's great work we have learned to call the Expansion of Christianity. Missions do come in here and there, but usually by way of an appendix, or where some specially sensational missionary enterprise for a moment attracts attention, just as in text-books of systematic theology missions might rate a condescending page or two in the section on practical theology, instead of being recognized as the framework within which the whole of theology needs to be considered.

What is required is a basic reconsideration of what we are trying to do, when we study or teach Church history. Our theme must be seen as the story of the way of God among the nations of the earth; a story which begins with the call of Abraham to be the father of a chosen people, and which will continue until the second coming of Christ and the end of the age. This is the story of the Church, not as an enclosed and segregated entity, but as a dynamic power, in dialogue or conflict with all the religions and all the cultures upon earth. When so understood, it must surely become one of the most enthralling fields of investigation open to the enquiring mind of man.

Students of early Church history are probably more aware of this than they were. The Church is set against its environment, both Jewish and Graeco-Roman, and in such recent books as the study edited by Professor Momigliano of the conflict between Christianity and the non-Christian world in the fourth century, or Mr Brown's biography of Augustine, the intense intellectual and spiritual travail of the Church in that period comes alive. But then there is a long period in which the outside world tends to be forgotten. There is a reawakening of interest with the period of the great discoveries of the fifteenth and sixteenth centuries; but very soon our interest comes to be concentrated on the details of the Reformation, and the wider issues come to be forgotten.

If, however, we were to see our subject in its true proportions, the most exciting period of all arrives with the beginning of the nineteenth century and the vast missionary effort of all the Churches over the last hundred and fifty years. For, in that period, the Church for the first time entered into living contact, and this has sometimes meant intense conflict, with every non-Christian religion and every non-Christian culture, from the highly sophisticated civilization of the Chinese down to the elaborate, but from our point of view primitive, systems of living of the Australian aborigines. Almost without our being aware of it, the word 'Church' has taken on a dimension and a meaning unknown in previous ages. In the past, the term 'catholic' in its true sense could be used of the Church only proleptically, of faith and not of sight; today, the catholicity of the Church is visible, though still incomplete, in its extension throughout the entire world of men. This and no other is the Church to the study of the history of which we are by our profession committed.

THE SECULAR HISTORIANS TAKE A HAND

We may have been largely unaware of what has been happening. This has not been true of our colleagues in the world of profane history. If we do not wish to be left behind in the race, we shall have to look to our laurels.

It is most interesting to observe what has actually been happening in that other world of history. Until very recently secular historians dealt with the missionary enterprises of the Christian Church by simply ignoring them. It has often been noted that in the fourteen volumes of the first edition of the *Cambridge Modern History* there is only one reference to Christian missions, and that fortuitiously in connection with the great journeys in Africa of David Livingstone, who happened to be missionary as well as explorer. It is plain that that period of neglect is at an end.

The contrast between the old *Cambridge History* and the new is extremely instructive. In the volumes of the *New Cambridge Modern History* which deal with the period since 1850, the scholarly and conscientious writers cannot keep the missions out of the picture. At times I get the impression that these writers regard the missions as an irritating and intrusive element which ought not to be there, and which has hindered the natural development of historical process and the proper evolution of the peoples of Africa and Asia. But there the facts are, and these diligent students realize that to disregard them would result in a serious distortion of the picture which as historians they are pledged to present as truly as they can.

In the most recent times of all, some historians not pledged to any personal loyalty to the Christian faith or to any preconceived opinion in favour of the Christian mission have come to recognize almost unwillingly that that enterprise has been one of the great creative forces through which the modern world has come to be what it is. To me it was extremely interesting to read, in an excellent *African Outline* by a writer who betrays no special sympathy with missionaries and their work, Professor Paul Bohannan, the following sentences:

The great debt that Africa owes to missionaries is that in a situation in which the forces of trade, colonial government and the missions themselves were creating cultural havoc, it was only the missions that began to rebuild, and gave them a chance to rebuild. Whatever any individual Westerner may think of the missionary edifice, every African knows that it is to missionaries that they owe the beginning of the African educational system.[1]

That is good historical observation, all the more deserving of respect that it comes from one who can be regarded as impartial in the matter.

This being so, it is not surprising that for some of the best recent work in this field we have to turn not to the professionals but to those who come to missionary problems from outside. Let me give one or two examples.

As one of the most distinguished books in the field I would select Professor C. R. Boxer's *Christian Century in Japan, 1549–1650* (Cambridge 1951), a first-rate piece of thorough, competent and accurate historical research. The story is, of course, one of quite exceptional interest; the early Jesuits were among the first westerners to reside in Japan, and their observations are of first-class importance as a historical source. But what interested me as I read the book was that, though Professor Boxer comes to the theme primarily through his interest in the achievements of the Portuguese overseas, gradually the actors impose themselves

[1] English edition (London 1966), p. 216.

on him through their sincerity and courage, and the chapters which deal with the great persecution in which the first Japanese Church was destroyed rise to the height of noble tragedy.

In a very different field, Professor J. S. Webster, of the Department of History in the University of Ibadan, has opened up for us the story of *The African Churches among the Yoruba 1888–1922* (Oxford 1964). In 1864 Samuel Adjai Crowther had been consecrated as the first African bishop of the Anglican Church. Why, on his death in 1892, in defiance of African opinion, was a European successor appointed? Why were more than sixty years allowed to elapse before an African was again entrusted with full responsibility for a diocese? Professor Webster skilfully elucidates the various factors and points of view that played their part in these decisions, and in the strains which led to the formation of an independent African Church which persists to the present day. I am inclined to think that he underestimates the difficulties by which the missionaries were faced, and is rather hard on them. But he has shown convincingly the need for careful studies of these areas and periods in which Christianity has been one of the dominating factors in the contacts and conflicts between the West and those peoples which we are sometimes inclined patronizingly to dismiss as primitive.

A great deal of this kind of work is actually going on outside the ranks of professional Church historians. I was delighted to learn from Professor Terence Ranger of University College, Dar-es-Salaam, that one younger scholar is deeply engaged in research into the early history of the Scottish missions in Malawi, and that another is at work on a biography of Archdeacon Owen. Owen may not be even a name to the majority of my hearers, but in my Cambridge days he was very well known to Christians. Those were the days of intense controversy over Kenya and the claim of the settlers to 'self-government', which of course meant settler government for the benefit of the settlers. Owen was one of that remarkable group of militant Christians, as a result of whose labours the British government was persuaded in 1923 to make its notable declaration that Kenya is African territory, and that, in the event of any clash between the interests of different sections of the population, the interests of the African must prevail. It will be good to have details of that exciting time set out in full on the basis of scientific research.

With so much activity in the world of the secular historians, it is clear that those of us who are specially concerned with the history of the Church and of Christian ideas will have to take a fresh look at our responsibilities, if we are not to be completely left behind. I would like to suggest certain stretches of the subject in which a great deal remains to be done, and in which perhaps we by reason of our special interests ought to be intensively engaged.

THINGS THAT NEED TO BE DONE

1. There are some astonishing gaps in periods of history which are fairly well but rather superficially known.

The labours of Fr G. Schurhammer have provided us in two bulky volumes, to which a third remains to be added, with all that anyone could wish to know, and perhaps a little more, about Francis Xavier and his times. It is astonishing that we still wait for any fully satisfactory life of Robert de Nobili. When the centenary of de Nobili's death approached (1856–1956), Roman Catholic authorities very properly set about the task of commissioning a new and up-to-date life. Their choice fell on Mr Vincent Cronin, a journalist who would make no claim to be a theologian, but at whose disposal were placed documents perhaps never before available to a biographer of de Nobili. The result, *A Pearl to India* (London 1959), is highly readable, and does make available a certain amount of new information. But it could not by any possibility be regarded as serious history. Our best authority is still the work of Fr Dahmen which appeared nearly forty years ago.

It may be that this delay is providential. A new epoch in the study of the Madura Mission has been opened up by the publication in Tuticorin of a number of Tamil works of de Nobili which were known to exist, but which I for one had never seen. A first survey has been published in the *Bangalore Theological Forum*; this suggests that a somewhat radical reconsideration of de Nobili's position *vis à vis* the religions of India will have to be carried through; and, as these works are not likely to be translated, we shall be dependent on those who can read Tamil for fuller acquaintance with their contents.

2. Almost all missionary biographies need to be rewritten. A recent work on *British Baptist Missionaries in India 1793–1837* by E. D. Potts (Cambridge 1967) has shown how much material still lies unsorted in the archives of the time. But the principal impression derived by one reader is that this modern and careful work has added still further lustre to the reputation of that best of all missionary biographies, John Clark Marshman's *Life and Times of Carey, Marshman and Ward* (London 1859). Filial piety did sometimes lead the younger Marshman a little to overestimate the merits of his distinguished father; otherwise he maintained an astonishing objectivity and impartiality in his handling of a crucial period in Christian history.

The exception proves the rule. John Pollock, in his enchanting work *Hudson Taylor and Maria* (London 1962), has shown us what can be done by fresh work on rather well-known records of a not very distant time. The official life of Hudson Taylor, the founder of the China Inland Missions, by his son and daughter-in-law, is a classic; I have read and re-read it with immense profit. But we can now see just how delicately the warts were removed from the portrait, and a faint aura of sanctity diffused over all the comings and goings of a man who in real life did attain to a very high degree of Christian sanctity. (I have verified this in conversation with those who knew him.) Taylor emerges from the ordeal of critical study more human, and by no means diminished in stature as an apostle of modern times.

Apart from rewriting, there are still many gaps to be filled in. Foss Westcott, a son of the great bishop, was himself a bishop in India for more than forty years, and Metropolitan during the two great crises of the independence of the Church of India, Burma and Ceylon, and the formation of the Church of South India. Plans were made for a life; but when the biographer proposed for this work found that the family were insisting on a hagiographical portrait, he was not prepared to go any further, and the work remains undone. Westcott was a very great man, but like other Christians he had his faults, including a sharp temper and a caustic tongue. Harry Waller, the great Bishop of Madras (another unrecorded giant), once remarked that the consequence of Westcott's becoming absorbed in Moral Rearmament was that it was now possible to play tennis with him.

3. We greatly need a large number of area studies, dealing in depth with the impact of the Christian gospel on places and peoples, and the modifications that Christian method has itself undergone as a result of these contacts. Such studies must be fully ecumenical.

The gravest defect of missionary history in the past has been the total neglect of the ecumenical aspect. The remarkable four-volume work edited by Mgr Delacroix calls itself *Histoire universelle des missions catholiques* (Paris 1956 ff.), and we have therefore no right to complain that it carries out exactly the task indicated in its title. But the equally notable work of Mgr Muelders bears only the title *Missiegeschiedenis* (Bussum 1957) and makes hardly any mention of anything except Roman Catholic work. It must be stressed that, in this ecumenical age, any work dealing with Christian history in this manner is out of date before it has appeared from the press.

We can record a small number of really careful and thorough studies of particular regions. For instance Dr H. Debrunner's careful work *A Church between Colonial Powers: a Study of the Church in Togo* (London 1965) does meet most of our requirements for one small area, though strict criticism might affirm that this is rather material for history than history full-blown. The recent composite and thoroughly ecumenical work on the history of Christianity in the Philippines is full of promise, but suffers from the disjointed character that is common to all such works by many hands.

One aspect of the history to which in the past far too little attention has been paid is the interaction of missions and governments over almost the whole area where missionary work has been carried on. Bishop Birkeli, now Primate of Norway, and author of an excellent study of mission and politics in the early days in Madagascar, told me that much of his work was done in the Public Record Office in Chancery Lane, where are to be found acres of documents on this theme, which have never been looked at since they were stored away in that inexhaustible quarry of miscellaneous information.

Only when all this detailed work has been done will it be possible satisfactorily to rewrite that provisional survey of the whole field which I attempted to supply in my one-volume history of Christian missions.

4. Our Christian history has been written far too much from the side of the operators and far too little from that of the victims. 'The toad beneath the harrow knows...' We know fairly well what it feels like to be a missionary; we know much less of what it feels like to be the object of the missionary's attentions. What is the process through which the Gospel becomes first intelligible, then attractive, and finally overwhelming in its demands?

The only thorough study of this theme known to me is the great work of Professor R. Allier, *La Psychologie de la conversion chez les peuples primitifs* (Paris 1928). Allier started by working through all the files of the *Journal des missions évangeliques*, and made extraordinarily good use of what he found. But this work is already forty years old, and Allier was perhaps a little too much of a systematizer, using ready-made categories which he had taken over from the French psychologist Janet, a scholar whose fame has been somewhat unduly overshadowed by that of Sigmund Freud.

One must frankly recognize the difficulty in the way of history-writing from this angle. The vast majority of converts have been wholly inarticulate; something happened to them, but exactly what it was they have found themselves unable to relate. When they have given an account of their experiences, it has generally been in the pietistic phrases that they had learned from their missionary friends. There are some exceptions. Dewan Bahadur Appasamy Pillai, long recognized as the doyen of South Indian Christians and the father of distinguished sons, among them Bishop A. J. Appasamy of Coimbatore, has left behind an intelligent autobiography under the title *Fifty Years'*

Pilgrimage of a Convert (Madras 1924). Similar records must exist in a number of languages. The trouble is that much of the material is to be found in periodicals not easily available, and in many cases in languages not readily accessible to the scholar. My predecessor, Bishop Western, was successful in securing a complete set of the *Narpothagam*, the monthly periodical put out in Tamil by the missionaries for more than eighty years—a remarkable periodical; I somewhat startled the Lambeth Conference of 1948 by mentioning that Butler's *Analogy of Religion* had been translated into Tamil and published in monthly instalments in the years 1858–9 for the edification of the village catechists! South Indian Christians are not as ignorant and unwary as some of the assembled Fathers had imagined them to be! I fancy that, if one had time to work through this long series of volumes, and others like it, much first-hand material would come to light. But this, once again, is a work that must be accomplished by specialists in many areas and in many tongues, before any attempt can be made at a satisfactory synthesis.

5. In the last section I was speaking of the other end of the Christian telescope. It must not, however, be forgotten that there is also the aspect of hostile observation and criticism of the missionary enterprise on the part of those who condemned it root and branch and wished for nothing less than its extermination.

We owe an immense debt to Origen for preserving for us so much of the actual writing of Celsus. We see the old world threatened by this new dynamic movement, against which it was hard put to it to find adequate weapons for defence. The same sense of danger echoes through all the long controversies about the Altar of Victory in Rome. Is it possible for us to hear the point of view of the other side in this history which we have tended to view only through Christian eyes?

The only book known to me that specifically deals with this subject is the remarkable work of Paul A. Cohen, *China and Christianity: the Missionary Movement and the Growth of Chinese Anti-foreignism* (Cambridge, Mass. 1963), in which excellent use has been made of Chinese sources. For the first time it has become possible for the Western reader to understand the extreme venom and viciousness of the anti-Christian propaganda put out by educated Chinese; we are, I think, in a better position to understand some of the complexities of the Christian situation in China today.

For India we have excellent information as to the major anti-Christian movement—the Arya Samaj founded by Devanand Sarasvati in 1875, one of the principal aims of which was and is the reconversion of Hindus who have been so incautious as to allow themselves to be converted by Christian missionaries. A number of careful studies have been made of this movement, and the principal texts are available in English. I am inclined to think, however, that a considerable pamphlet war was carried on for the best part of a century. I saw recently an interesting collection of Christian tracts in English, mainly written by Indian authors and published in 1870 by the famous Dr Murdoch of the Christian Literature Society (none giving any trace of that scurrility by which Christian controversial literature is supposed to have been marked). It would be interesting to know whether any corresponding collection has been made of Hindu and Muslim answers. One point that has recently come to my attention is that anti-Christian controversialists in India were aided by Bradlaugh and other rationalists in Britain. This is a subject which it would be most interesting to follow up. The full-blooded Victorians were much less inhibited by the rules of moderation and courtesy than their feebler descendants.

6. So far we have been thinking of the main lines of missionary advance; in recent years we have become increasingly aware of the significance of what may be called the side-lines. This is true of the study of Church history as a whole; movements such as that of the Anabaptists which used to be treated as simply heretical have now been promoted to respectability as the Radical Reformation, in its way no less significant and fruitful than the other currents of reform in the sixteenth century. We may have to undertake a similar extensive rethinking of what has been happening all over the world as a result of Christian missionary activity.

The area to which most attention has been directed is that of the so-called African splinter churches. In the past missionaries have on the whole taken a low view of such movements, as divisive, syncretistic, and superstitious. A new epoch began with the first edition of Bishop Sundkler's now famous book *Bantu Prophets in South Africa* (second edition, Oxford 1961). To this must now be added Professor H. W. Turner's remarkable study of the Aladura Church in Nigeria and elsewhere, and Dr D. B. Barrett's comprehensive survey. This is an extraordinarily complex field; the innumerable Christian and quasi-Christian movements cannot be reduced to one single common denominator; but all who have worked seriously on the problem are now in agreement that here we are face to face with a phenomenon deserving of the most careful study; some would go so far as to speak of it as a genuine African reformation, an attempt to arrive at an African confrontation with the Gospel, without the confusions introduced into the African apprehension by the Western mind. The Kimbanguist Church in the Congo claims a million members and shows every sign of becoming a stable and well-organized community; we shall be in possession of much fuller information about its recent developments when Mlle Dr M. L. Martin has completed the studies on which she is now engaged.

In this and the kindred field of the so-called Cargo-cults in the South Sea the sociologists have had a fine time of it. What were the causes that produced almost simultaneously over widely separated areas this phenomenon of millennial expectation, in which somewhat garbled ideas drawn from the New Testament are mingled with a reversion to tribal memories and rites, and the hope of an immediate reversal of all things, in which the black man will come into his rights and the white man will be overthrown? A large literature has grown up over the last few years; it is to be regretted that so little of it is theological or in the strict sense of the term historical.

By this and similar routes we are introduced to one of the most fundamental questions of all—that of the impact of the Gospel on races which are newly introduced to it with little or no preparation. I have elsewhere put forward the view that for the theological student in Africa and similar areas the most important period of Church history is that of the so-called Dark Ages, during which the Church was wrestling for the first time with many of the problems that recur with startling similarity in many parts of the world today. What are the strains and tensions which are set up in the mind and soul of a rapidly Christianized people? How can these strains be kept within bounds, and what are the lessons that we can learn from the past?

Of course the missionaries have not been alone in producing the contemporary situation; their presence has been mixed up with that of traders and administrators and ethnologists, but they have certainly played a leading part in the exposure of these peoples to Western ideas. The event which has naturally attracted most attention has been the Mau Mau rising in Kenya, where the white victims of the frenzy were remarkably few, the vast majority of those killed having been Africans who would not go along. What was the nature of what seems almost to have been a neurosis by which a whole people was affected? What were the various forces that combined to produce the crisis? It would be facile to look for ready-made Freudian explanations of the situation and of the reactions of Africans to it. But no simple explanation will do. Why was it that only one tribe, the Kikuyu, were affected, and that the disturbance did not spread? What was it that made so many Christians refuse to take the Mau Mau oath, even though they knew perfectly well that death was likely to follow on their refusal?

The historian may be inclined to say that this lies outside his province. I am not sure that I would agree. We understand history in a broader sense than some of our forebears; it is hard to draw the line between history and sociology; and, if we regard the study of human motive as part of our concern, we cannot exclude the new insights of psychological research, though we may be far more cautious in our use of them than those experts who think that they can find a scientific explanation for all the twists and turns of the argument of *Alice in Wonderland*.

7. One more area, and I am done. In our last section we were thinking primarily of those who have come directly within the sphere of the Church, and have then left it to make their own

adventure of faith and expression elsewhere. There is another and kindred sphere—that of those who have never become Christians, but whose thought and understanding of life show plain evidences of the attraction of the Gospel and in particular of the figure of Jesus Christ. There has been much discussion lately, especially in the Roman Catholic Church, of the 'limits of the Church'. Once the subject is seriously considered, we realize that the Church is like the sun. Look at it through a piece of smoked glass and it appears to have as firm and clear an outline as a shilling (or should I now say five new pence?). See it as the astronomer sees it, at the time of a total eclipse, and we realize that the corona shoots out many millions of miles into space. In view of what we know of the generosity of God, it will not surprise us that something like this is a true picture of the Church as it really is.

One of the new concepts that meets us in much contemporary writing is that of the latent Church, propagated by among others Professor Hoekendijk, of Union Seminary, New York. The term is not perfectly clear, but useful in this connection. For instance, those who know Japan tell us that, though the number of registered Christians of all denominations is less than one per cent of the population, the Bible continues to be in a remarkable way a best-seller, and it seems clear that there is a large section of the population which is Christian rather than anything else.

Much can be learned from a study of the non-Christian apologists for other faiths, whose apologies seem to a considerable extent to be determined by their contacts with the Christian faith which they have never accepted. Mahatma Gandhi made no secret of his interest in the New Testament and his admiration for Jesus Christ. Professor Radhakrishnan displays at all times an astonishing acquaintance with Christian theology. Aurobindo Ghose was educated entirely in England and must have come closely in contact with Christian circles. When men of this stature set forth their understanding of Hinduism, how far is the picture drawn from the Hindu classics, and how far is the texture in reality Christian, though the cloth is presented as genuine Hindu weave? And how does all this fit into the picture of the historical process of the interlocking of different cultures and traditions in the increasingly unified world of our day?

Much good work has been done in this field. Dr Otto Wolff, in his *Christus unter den Hindus* (1966), has presented a very sympathetic picture of these thinkers, in their endeavour to do justice both to what they have learned of Jesus Christ and to the traditions to which they still proclaim their loyalty. Perhaps Dr Wolff has been led by sympathy a little to underestimate the real differences which subsist between even the most liberal interpretation of Christianity and the most Christianized version of Hinduism or Islam; but his work is of value because based on original sources and on a real effort to get inside the minds of those who had been led to a serious confrontation with the Christian faith. There is much still to be done in India as well as in other countries in this direction.

Here then are the seven areas in which advancement of knowledge is both possible and desirable. And when that has been done, though of course it never can be done in a permanent and unalterable form, the time will come for synthesis, for the putting together of all assured results from the diverse and often minute pieces of detailed research into one coherent picture. For this, of course, we shall have to wait for the emergence of the genius who has that special and rare gift of drawing together scattered lights into one clear radiance, of taking detail seriously, yet without distortion of the general proportions without regard for which a picture becomes a caricature. I am not here referring to a new *History of Missions* more ample and more accurate because based on knowledge which is not now available. I am fully aware that, in twenty years' time, my own short *History of Christian Missions* (Harmondsworth 1964) will need such extensive revision as to be no longer the same book. I am thinking of something far more significant for Christian faith and knowledge —a presentation of the Christian faith in the new and wider perspectives that come to us when we see it as what it is today— a more universal faith than has ever previously existed among the sons of men, with the beginnings of that process by which the riches of all the nations will be gathered into the city of God.

The history of missions

I suppose that many of us would agree that Edwyn Bevan's little sketch of *Christianity* in the Home University Library (London 1933) is the best thing in that vein that has ever been done. Bevan brought to the task the minutely accurate information of the scholar, together with no mean gifts of style and the artist's perception of proportion and grouping. But that admirable book is still basically Western; it shows awareness of larger dimensions, but it was written in the pre-ecumenical age, and any writer is conditioned by the time and place in which he lived. It may be that the new Bevan needed for our age is not yet born, or has not yet emerged from his swaddling-clothes. I do not see him in the ranks of existing historians of missions; this may simply mean that his time is not yet come.

THE WAY FORWARD

This lays upon us the duty to do all that can be done in the next twenty or thirty years to make sure that this vitally important part of Church history is better cultivated and more sedulously studied than in the past.

We have to face the fact that it is not easy to find students willing to undertake research in the field of missions and of the confrontation of beliefs and cultures in the modern world, unless it be disguised under the blessed name of sociology. In England hardly any work of first-rate value in this field has appeared from the universities; Professor Owen Chadwick's excellent study *Mackenzie's Grave* (London 1959) is a shining exception; but this was the work of a mature and accomplished historian, and not of a young man making his début in the world of learning. In Germany fields of research are rather strictly specialized, and the career which an aspiring academic may hope to follow is largely determined by the subject which he chooses for his doctorate dissertation. In consequence, though it would be possible without difficulty to suggest fifty subjects which urgently need to be worked out in the field of missions, too many candidates for doctorates will still choose to write on some obscure theologian of the seventeenth or eighteenth century, of whom no one has ever heard, and of whom no one would particularly wish to hear. The most hopeful spot in the landscape seems at the moment to be Uppsala, where Bishop Sundkler, not merely continuing his own researches, has managed to gather round him a group of enterprising students. Dr Sharpe's study of J. N. Farquhar,[1] and Dr Hallencreutz's study of Hendrik Kraemer[2] up to the publication of Kraemer's *The Christian Mission in a non-Christian world* (London 1938) are both valuable additions to the library of missionary studies.

At one point our position is much stronger than it was a generation ago. Today, representatives of the Younger Churches are beginning to study their own past; and, though contributions on the highest academic level are still few, what there are give promise of a much richer harvest in the future.

The first work of great historical value by a Younger-Church writer known to me is the study by Judge P. Cheriyan of the crisis in the relations between the Syrian Christians and the Church Missionary Society in the period between 1816 and 1840; this is based on a careful study of many original documents in a judicious and temperate spirit; some documents which Cheriyan had not seen are now available, and his work has to be modified in certain respects. But, for the period at which it was written, it is a highly commendable piece of work. It is encouraging that the younger generation of Nigerian historians, Professor Ajayi and others, are recognizing the great creative function which the missions performed in their country, and are looking at the past with critical but not hypercritical eyes.

At the same time Roman Catholics in the Younger Churches are also taking up the study both of the remoter and of the more recent past. To mention only one outstanding example, Fr de la Costa's account of the Jesuits in the Philippines, which has so far reached only the period of the dissolution of the Order, is a quite outstanding piece of historical research. The wealth of the material available may be realized from the fact that this large book deals with the work of only one religious Order in

---

[1] E. J. Sharp, *Not to destroy but to fulfil* (Uppsala 1965).
[2] C. F. Hallencreutz, *Kraemer towards Tambaram* (Uppsala 1966).

one country. But Fr de la Costa has worked on a scale large enough to enable us to see deeply into the daily lives and recurrent problems of the missionaries; the modern reader may be surprised to learn that one of the subjects most earnestly discussed among them was the use of chocolate by the Fathers; at one time the consumption of this highly stimulating drink was held to be dangerous to their virtue, but a later age came to think that its use might be permitted in moderate quantities.

The Asian or African historian has advantages, especially where a knowledge of non-European languages is required, but at times he is too close to the events which he records for a purely objective handling of the material to be possible. There is still a place for the Western scholar and student in this still largely unexplored and inexhaustible field of study.

The teacher of Church history in the West has a certain duty to point out to those wishing to engage in research that there are possibilities in the area of missionary history of which he may well be unaware. My main concern, however, in offering this paper to the Society is that we should look again both at the way in which we present Church history to our hearers, and at the way in which we ourselves understand it. Most of our time must be spent on limited enquiries into the problems of special fields; but even the detailed work cannot be well done, unless we have a clear picture of the whole. When, as I have pleaded, Church history comes to be understood as the entire history of the world seen in the light of a divine purpose, when the story of the Church is understood as the story of the way of God among the nations, it becomes an exciting discipline, and even the detail is lighted up by the splendour of that great whole to which it is related.

The qualifications required for the pursuit of knowledge in this area are the same as those demanded in any field of academic study. There must be, first, unwearied patience, since the material to be worked through is in many cases of such formidable dimensions. There must be adherence to the most rigorous critical method, in order to avoid the distortions of which I have spoken earlier in this paper. Perhaps we may venture to add as a qualification a sincere and humble Christian faith. The non-believer may bring to the work a certain objectivity such as we find it hard to maintain. On the other hand, he is debarred from understanding many of the subtler factors which play their part in every situation in which faith and the proclamation of the faith are concerned. We have this advantage over him that we see the whole of our work in the light of our faith, and are aware that, even in our dull and often trivial labours, we are trying to glorify God and to set forth some of the wonders of his operations among the sons of men.